Predator

The Unofficial Guide to the Movie Franchise

Nick Naughton

Contents

PREFACE

The Predator franchise is sometimes seen as a poor relation to the Alien series. 20th Century Fox certainly seemed to put more money into the Alien series than they did Predator but that was understandable because Alien and Aliens were both hugely popular and influential and remain pop culture touchstones. The Alien franchise, for two films at least, was always quite prestigious. Predator was always slightly more of a niche franchise than Alien and none of the Predator movies can be described as blockbusters or pop culture giants - though the first one was very profitable. The Predator franchise was always seen as somewhat more low-brow - presumably because these are essentially action films which then incorporate some horror and sci-fi elements. That's really the genius of the first Predator film though. It plays like an action war picture at first and then suddenly takes a sharp turn into horror and sci-fi.

Both of these famous Fox film franchises were eventually forced to suffer the indignity of the Alien vs Predator interlude - which thankfully had the plug rapidly pulled after the truly atrocious Aliens vs. Predator: Requiem. The Predator franchise - happily - did return in more undiluted fashion after this and proved with Prey that it still has plenty of life and potential left in it yet.

There is often a common misconception with the Predator franchise that, up until Prey, all the sequels were terrible. I don't agree with this perception at all. I love Predator 2 and Predators is a film that has somewhat grown on me over the years. Neither of these films are bad sequels at all if you ask me and I'll have plenty to say about both movies in this book. For my money the only real out and out clunker among the 'undiluted' Predator sequels is 2018's The Predator - in which Shane Black, for reasons best known to himself, seemed to think he was making an action comedy rather than an action horror film.

We'll discuss all of these films in this book and we shall also - of course - discuss the two AvP movies too. We'll look at the background of each film, the development of them, and discuss worked and what didn't in the actual movie. The Predators themselves remain an intriguing and fearsome movie antagonist. Their physical attributes, advanced technology, and unique culture make them both frightening and mysterious. Yet, it is the Predators' culture that truly fascinates. These enigmatic aliens who come to Earth on safari. They view themselves as apex predators and seek worthy adversaries to engage in one-on-one combat.

Through elaborate rituals and tests of skill, they carefully choose targets that display exceptional strength, intelligence, or combat ability. Inspired by their intense dedication to the hunt, they have developed a vast array of weaponry. Energy-based plasma cannons, razor-sharp retractable blades, deadly nets, high-tech spears, and throwable explosive devices are just a few examples of their arsenal. What sets the Predators apart from mindless killers, however, is their strict code of honour. Instead of overwhelming their targets, they prefer to engage in fair one-on-one combat - even toying with their prey at times rather than kill them straight away.

This sense of honour and celebration of the hunt distinguishes them as complex beings, transcending the realm of mere villains. The Predators are fearsome and frightening but what makes them especially chilling is that they are smart and cunning. These creatures have mastered space travel so they are clearly way more intelligent than us. If you ever encounter a Predator you are most likely toast. They are not unbeatable though. A few brave souls have gone up against a Predator and lived to tell the tale. The book that follows will tell you all about them.

PREDATOR (1987)

Predator is said to have started life as a flippant joke about Rocky Balboa having to fight an alien in the next film because he'd beaten everyone else. Jim and John Thomas, brothers from California, wrote the first script treatment - which was originally called The Hunter and then simply Hunter. The first script for The Hunter was written in a single weekend. The main concept of Hunter was that a highly advanced and lethal alien comes to Earth to hunt humans - in the same way that humans (well, those who are cruel and heartless enough anyway) go on safari to hunt animals in Africa.

It struck the Thomas brothers that if a deadly alien did come to Earth to hunt humans the people it hunted would have to be heavily armed military types because otherwise the 'hunt' wouldn't be much of a challenge for the alien. The pulpy sci-fi script, which obviously owed something to Alien but actually predated Aliens (despite its similar military v aliens premise), would be revised many times before Predator hit the screen.

In the original Hunter script there was going to be a party of aliens hunting on Earth but later revisions later changed this so there was a single Predator. The formula of having a single Predator hunting humans seems to be the one that works best in Predator movies. When they try to introduce more Predators or mess around with the Predator too much it never quite seems to work as well. New Zealand filmmaker Geoff Murphy was the original director on Predator. Murphy was best known for the cult sci-fi film The Quiet Earth. He later directed Hollywood films like Young Guns II and Under Siege 2: Dark Territory and was a second unit director on Peter Jackson's Lord of the Rings films. Murphy developed the Hunter script for a time with Jim and John Thomas but some of his ideas clashed with the studio 20th Century Fox.

Murphy wanted the alien hunter to be patently female and also wanted a sequence where the military team destroy a rebel camp in the jungle and kill everyone but then find it was being defended by boys and old men - who they've now just slaughtered. The studio obviously chafed at this last suggestion in particular. They felt Murphy was being a bit too radical, political even, for a sci-fi actioner. They wanted Hunter to be a sci-fi action film - not a gritty anti-war drama or critique of American foreign policy!

Geoff Murphy had Harrison Ford in mind for the lead in Hunter and wanted James Woods to play the untrustworthy CIA man foisted on the military team. It seems rather doubtful that Harrison Ford, then at the peak of his career, would have actually agreed to be in the film but you never know. His fee alone would have taken a fair chunk out of the budget! The fact that Murphy wanted James Woods in the film too was an indication of how he viewed the movie differently from the producers. The roles in Predator would eventually be taken by larger than life action stars and James Woods, though a terrific actor, was definitely not an action star.

Joel Silver then came onboard as a producer and told Geoff Murphy that Arnold Schwarzenegger was going to be the lead in Hunter. In fact, there was already a deal in place where if Schwarzenegger's 1985 film Commando had a big opening he would get the part. Commando opened big and Arnold was cast in Hunter (as it was back then). Schwarzenegger hadn't actually made that many films at the time and wasn't taken very seriously as an actor. As far as action stars went, Sly Stallone was still the top dog and Arnie was some way behind. It was the double impact of Commando and Predator (and also the big box-office numbers of the 1988 comedy film Twins) which lifted Schwarzenegger up into Hollywood superstardom. By the early nineties, Arnold was headlining blockbuster films like Total Recall and Terminator 2 and had become a bigger star than Stallone.

Geoff Murphy really disliked the casting of Arnold Schwarzenegger as the lead in Hunter and complained to the studio. Murphy wanted the lead to be an all American GI type and said that Arnold Schwarzenegger could barely speak English! Geoff Murphy thought that Arnold was a terrible actor and would hobble any ambitions he had to make Hunter a credible film about plausible military men (plausible military men who just happen to find themselves up against an alien!). Nonetheless, despite his unhappiness, Murphy agreed to work with Arnold on the film and accept the casting. However, what Murphy didn't know was that, as part of his deal for signing on, Schwarzenegger had a say in the choice of director on Hunter.

Word got back to Arnie that Geoff Murphy had complained about him being cast in Hunter so Schwarzenegger asked for Murphy to be replaced by John McTiernan. In his memoir, Murphy said - "That is how I blew probably the biggest break I could have got in Hollywood. It was my big mouth!" There is actually another oft told story concerning why Arnold didn't want Geoff Murphy to direct Hunter. A few years before, Murphy was one of the directors interviewed about doing a proposed third Conan the Barbarian film with Schwarzenegger. During his interview Murphy had, as a joke, referred to the character as Conan the Librarian. Arnold apparently didn't think this was very funny.

Suffice to say then, Arnold didn't appear to be the biggest Geoff Murphy fan in the world. There is an alternate universe out there somewhere where Predator was directed by Geoff Murphy but we'll never know how that film might have turned out. The choice of John McTiernan to direct the film was amazingly shrewd in hindsight. At the time McTiernan had only directed one film. This was Nomads - a baffling supernatural thriller with Pierce Brosnan. Schwarzenegger said he was impressed though by the sense of atmosphere in Nomads that he knew McTiernan was the right choice to direct Hunter.

John McTiernan was more than happy to accept the job on Hunter. McTiernan took the art of direction very seriously and soon had plenty of his own ideas about what sort of film Hunter should be. Another change, besides hiring a new director, that Schwarzenegger instigated was that he didn't want the film to be him versus the alien for too much of its running time - as was proposed in the early drafts. He wanted more of a Wild Bunch/Dirty Dozen scenario. Schwarzenegger wanted to be part of an ensemble where the other actors were just as imposing and rugged as him. At some point the plan to call the film Hunter was changed and the title settled on Predator. Hunter always seemed a trifle generic as a title and Predator was much more inspired.

Carl Weathers, who was of course best known for the Rocky films, was always the first choice for Dillon. Weathers, for some reason, never became a film star in his own right - though he did make an attempt the following year when he was the lead in Action Jackson, a (as the title implies!) action film directed by Craig R. Baxley. Baxley was the second unit director on Predator. Action Jackson was not a hit and Weathers did a lot of television instead - appearing in shows like Tour of Duty and Street Justice.

Carl Weathers is brilliant in Predator and more than makes the most of the part of Dillon. Weathers is great casting because not only is he beefy enough to share the screen with Schwarzenegger he's also a terrific actor. In fact, when it comes to acting and plot, it is Weathers who does much of the heavy lifting in Predator.

The mean looking 6'4 Bill Duke, who was in Commando with Arnold, was cast as Mac. Duke was actually more of a director until Commando. He had directed on many TV shows like Dallas, Hill Street Blues, Matlock, and Cagney & Lacy. Bill Duke became good friends with Arnold on Commando and so was asked to be in Predator. Duke played a baddie in Commando and had a memorable fight with Arnie in that film. Sonny Landham, who usually played villains, was cast as the spiritual Native American soldier Billy. Landham was half Cherokee and one-eighth Seminole descent. Landham began his career in erotic films but had become a mainstream actor by now. He had supporting roles in films like The Warriors and 48 Hrs. Landham was also in the 1985 television movie The Dirty Dozen: Next Mission - which must have been good preparation to play in a military themed ensemble like Predator.

The insurance company insisted that Sonny Landham could only be hired if he was given a bodyguard. "Not to protect Sonny, but to protect other people from Sonny," said John McTiernan. Landham was a famed loose cannon away from the camera. "On the weekends when we weren't working," said Bill Duke, "we would sometimes go to these clubs. We're having a good time at this club. And then we didn't know where Sonny was, and it got us worried because sometimes you got a little drunk, whatever. And so, I forgot who it is, [someone] went, "Look over there, look over there!" Sonny is on the floor, crawling around the floor, and either he was touching or kissing women's legs. On the dance floor. I think that's when they called the security guy to be with him."

Shane Black plays Hawkins, the commando team's bespectacled radio operator. Black was a screenwriter and had recently written Lethal Weapon and The Monster Squad at the time. Black was given a supporting actor role in the film by 20th Century Fox so they would have someone at the heart of the production to keep an eye on the inexperienced director John McTiernan and the script. Black later directed the fourth film in the franchise - The Predator. Shane Black later said that he refused to do any writing on the set of Predator because he had been hired as an actor and wanted to focus on that. John Davis, the producer, said that because of Black refusing to do rewrites of the script they killed off the character of Hawkins first! Black did say though that he contributed the jokes which Hawkins tells Billy in the film.

Jesse Ventura, a former wrestler and Navy veteran, was cast as Blain. The firing speed of the M134 Minigun (Ol' Painless) used by Jesse Ventura in Predator was reduced by the production crew because the director wanted the audience to see the barrels spin. Ol' Painless was so heavy to pick up that the actors could only carry it for a few minutes at a time. The same year that Predator came out, Ventura was also in The Running Man with Arnold Schwarzenegger. Arnold Schwarzenegger had gym equipment sent to the set of Predator in Mexico from the United States so that the actors could work out during the shoot. It became something of a competition between Arnie, Ventura, and Carl Weathers to see who could do the most gym work. Jesse Ventura said he was delighted when he learned he had bigger arms than Schwarzenegger! Ventura was still wrestling at the time and actually took a break from the Predator shoot at one point to take part in a wrestling match back in the United States.

Richard Chaves, who plays Poncho in Predator, was a real life Vietnam veteran. Chaves was often cast as police officers or military men. Shortly after Predator, Chaves was cast in the TV show The War of the Worlds - which serves as a sequel of sorts to the 1953 film. Richard Chaves plays the no nonsense military man Ironhorse in War of the Worlds. Sadly, Chaves was killed off at the start of season two and replaced by Adrian Paul. Richard Chaves was cast in Predator because the producers saw him in a play called Tracers. Chaves had just failed an audition for a small part in the John Landis comedy movie Three Amigos! when he got the part of Poncho.

The great R. G. Armstrong has a small part in Predator as as Major General Homer Philips. John McTiernan said Armstrong was a bit old for the part but he just wanted him in the film so didn't worry about this too much. The Mexican actress Elpidia Carrillo was cast as Anna, the insurgent the team reluctantly takes as a prisoner. Elpidia Carrillo had been in films like Under Fire and Salvador. Carrillo said it was quite an experience being the only woman in the cast of this macho action film!

Although they were never mentioned in the final film, the full names of the main characters in the original script Were Major Alan "Dutch" Schaefer, SSG George Dillon, Sergeant Mac Eliot, Sergeant Blain Cooper, Sergeant Billy Sole, Corporal Poncho Ramirez and Corporal Rick Hawkins. A slightly bizarre piece of Predator trivia is that two members of the cast (Arnold Schwarzenegger and Jessie Ventura) went into politics and became Governors. Sonny Landham tried (and failed) to make it a hat trick when he ran in the Republican Party primary election for the post of Governor of Kentucky.

The song which plays as the team fly over the jungle in a helicopter at the start is Long Tall Sally. Long Tall Sally is a rock and roll song written by Robert "Bumps" Blackwell, Enotris Johnson, and Little Richard. It was originally performed by Little Richard and released as a single in 1956. The song has since become a classic and has been covered by various artists over the years. The song was later used in the closing credits for Predators.

Predator was shot in 1986 in Mexico. Palenque, Chiapas, and Mismaloya were used as locations. The Misol-Ha waterfall was used for the sequence where Dutch jumps in the water. Misol-Ha Waterfall lies in the Chiapas region of Mexico. The film had a $15 million budget. It was quite a troubled production - for one thing the script was still being rewritten as production began. Each morning there were new hastily written scenes. Arnold Schwarzenegger said that making the film was something of an endurance test. It was stiflingly hot during the day and then freezing cold at other times. They warmed Arnold up on the set by giving him Jagertee. Jagertee is a popular Austrian alcoholic beverage made with black tea, rum, red wine, and various spices such as cinnamon, cloves, and orange peel. Arnold said that he had to brave leech infested water on more than one occasion during the shoot.

Over the course of Predator, you can see Schwarzenegger's character Dutch start to look a bit gaunt. This is because Schwarzenegger got ill eating the local Mexican food and so stopped eating (as much as he could). He did one scene with an IV bottle in his arm. The cast and crew all lost a huge amount of weight when it dawned on them that the local food and water wasn't safe. John McTiernan lost 25 pounds shooting Predator because he refused to eat the local Mexican food. Bill Duke said that there were a lot of bugs and mosquitoes in the food - which obviously didn't do too much for anyone's appetite. After his experience on Predator, Schwarzenegger hired a personal chef for all his movies.

Predator also seemed to put Arnie off shooting movies abroad. He was supposed to make a Sgt. Rock movie (Sgt. Rock is the comic book Hawkins is reading in the Predator end credits) in the early 1990s but bailed out when he learned it was going to be shot in Southeast Europe. After his experience on Predator, Arnold decided he wanted to make his films in California so that he could go home and eat dinner with his family at night. Schwarzenegger actually took a break from shooting Predator to get married. On April 26, 1986, Schwarzenegger married Maria Shriver in Hyannis, Massachusetts. The honeymoon was only two days long because Arnold had to get back to the Predator set.

It was something of a miracle that such a memorable monster emerged in Predator in the end because the film started shooting with a completely different Predator design. Martial arts star Jean Claude Van Damme (then completely unknown) had been hired to play the Predator (the thinking was that his athleticism would make the alien appear quick and formidable) and the alien costume he was given looked like a cross between a fly, a prawn and a dog with big yellow eyes and spindly legs like stilts. Boss Film Studios, owned by Richard Edlund, designed the first alien costume. The original concept was that the alien would be fast and be able to move through trees like a monkey. The alien costume just didn't work though. The suit looked like a monster from Space 1999. It wasn't iconic or scary at all.

"We needed two different Predator suits," said assistant director Beau Marks. "One is the suit that when you can see him and one's the suit where you couldn't see him, which was a kind of a hold-out suit. It was all red so when we shot it in the jungle we could pull a matte off of it. Probably a couple weeks before we needed the Predator a box comes. And we open it up and it looks like a giant red rubber chicken. It's pretty hard to have the most deadly alien from outer space coming to hunt man and it looks like a f—ing chicken unless you're doing a comedy. The real suit came shortly thereafter and it wasn't any better. So we shot some tests with it and it became quite obvious that this was a disaster." The 'red rubber chicken' suit was later an Easter egg in Shane Black's

2018 film The Predator. You can see someone dressed in a silly red monster suit during the Halloween sequence in that film.

The first costumes were atrocious and, after shooting a couple of sequences, John McTiernan sent the costumes back to the studio and told them the film would be a laughing stock if he carried on like this. When production was shut down, Arnold Schwarzenegger stepped in and asked special effects expert Stan Winston (with whom he had become friends while making The Terminator) if he could come up with anything to save the picture. Winston was inspired by illustrations of Rasterfarian warriors he'd seen and came up with a new Predator that had dreadlocks and a steel mask and looked much more like a fearsome warrior hunter than the other design.

One of the special effects people said that Jean Claude Van Damme appeared to be labouring under the impression that he was going to have a kung fu fight with Schwarzenegger at the end of the film! John McTiernan said of Van Damme - "It was a complete screw up with his agent, trying to hustle him into a job and didn't know what the movie was. It's silly. It was really silly." The diminutive Van Damme (who had done nothing but complain about the heat anyway) was jettisoned and they hired the 7 foot plus Kevin Peter Hall to play the Predator instead. The helicopter pilot at the end of the film is also Kevin Peter Hall.

Hall played a Yeti in Harry and the Hendersons (a comedy with John Lithgow) around the same time as Predator. Hall suffered from the heat in the Predator suit and could also barely see in the costume. He remained friendly and patient throughout the shoot though and was a gentle giant away from the camera. Having the Predator be 7 foot tall was clearly the right approach because it meant that - just for once - even the mighty Schwarzenegger looked like he was out of his depth.

The explosive and bombastic sequence in Predator where Dutch and his commando team destroy a rebel camp in the jungle was shot by second unit director Craig Baxley. John McTiernan disliked this sequence and tried to have it removed. McTiernan felt that it didn't really fit in with the tone of the rest of the movie. McTiernan also felt it was too 'static' and didn't conform to the directorial style he had used in the rest of the film. Baxley had shot the sequence because he felt they needed some spectacular footage to placate worried studio executives (who were threatening to shut the film down because it was going over budget). It eventually stayed in the film.

The jungle base sequence, which is like something out of The A-Team (Baxley actually worked on The A-Team) but on a much bigger budget and with much more violence, didn't mesh with the stoic and serious early tone John McTiernan had established but it is an awful lot of fun all the same. Predator just wouldn't be Predator without this explosive sequence. What this sequence does too is establish the teamwork of these men and showcase their individual skills. In a weird way, though this sequence is a tonal clash with McTiernan, it works within the overall story because it makes Dutch and his team look invincible. This makes their sudden vulnerability against the Predator more effective.

The big jungle base attack sequence required 100 Mexican extras. They had to spend two weeks rigging the location with explosives. No actual jungle was destroyed shooting this sequence because it was filmed on a patch of land that had been cleared out by a fire a few years before. By the way, John McTiernan had wanted Dutch and his team to enter the jungle by performing a HALO jump out of a plane. He obviously didn't his way on this and in the film they rappel down ropes a helicopter. They had to fly in leaves to the location because the leaves on the trees started to turn orange during the shoot and the trees also began to look threadbare. John McTiernan broke his wrist falling out of a tree during the shoot so you can't say that he didn't suffer for his art!

John McTiernan said that the scene in Predators where the soldiers shoot into the jungle for a couple of minutes (in the hope of hitting the Predator) was a vague attempt at a subtext about the public fascination with guns. "What I was really doing was to quietly ridicule the desire to see pictures of guns firing. All of this is sort of a moral separate peace here, and in order to do it I set up the circumstance where there were no human beings in front of the guns. In fact the point of all the firing was, as the man says as soon as they stop shooting, 'We hit nothing.' The whole point was the impotence of all the guns." McTiernan said the studio were complaining to him that in his rushes there didn't seem to much footage of the guns in the film so he came up with this sequence.

There was a going to be a scene in Predator where we see the injured alien attending to its wounds on its spaceship. The construction of a spaceship interior for this scene was deemed too expensive though and replaced with a scene where the Predator patches up its wounds in a tree instead. The Predator's blood in Predator was originally supposed to be orange but they decided it was easier to make it green. Starburst magazine actually had an article during the production of Predator which predicted the film was a disaster in the making. Happily, this turned out to be completely wrong as far as crystal ball gazing went. In fact, Predator is considered to be a genuine action movie classic. Val Verde is a fictional country which was used in Joel Silver films. It also featured in Die Hard 2.

Trivia - the dead Green Beret that Dutch finds is called Jim Hopper. This was later used as the name of David Harbour's character in the popular Netflix show Stranger Things. The town in Stranger Things is called Hawkins - another Predator Easter egg. The Predator species is known as the "Yautja" in the expanded universe and other media. The iconic Predator heat vision effect was partly achieved by using an infrared camera - but digital effects and layers of camera footage also had to be used. The inspiration for the Predator vision was apparently based on how a snake sees its prey. You could say that the Predator is more or less cheating by using heat vision! It gives the alien a huge advantage because you can't hide from it - even in a jungle.

REVIEW

Predator is a fun science fiction action horror film and the picture that more or less established Arnold Schwarzenegger as a superstar. In the late 1980s and early 1990s, Schwarzenegger was the biggest star in Hollywood. You think Dwayne Johnson is a big star today? Well, he is but Arnold was twice as famous as Dwayne Johnson in his day. The double whammy of Commando and Predator firmly established the Arnie screen persona and it is impossible to think of anyone else playing "Dutch" Schaefer. Stan Winston's memorable and fearsome Predator creatures are just as iconic as Arnie in the movie - which is no mean feat. Seven foot aliens with an ornate tribal appearance, dreadlocks and armoured masks who hunt humans for sport with an assortment of deadly weapons and some advanced technology at their disposal.

Predator is a product of the last great era of Hollywood action films - the eighties. A decade of bone crunching blood splattered foul mouthed blockbuster epics (Robocop, The Terminator, Die Hard, Commando) that wouldn't know what a PG-13 rating was if it skewered them with a spear and ripped their spinal column out to keep as a trophy (as the Predator is apt to do on occasion). The film begins with a canvas of stars before a spacecraft slowly appears (I always try and guess which star will turn into the spaceship and always get it wrong) and sends a small pod hurtling towards Earth to the enjoyably melodramatic strains of Alan Silvestri's stirring score.

That is more or less the extent of the Predator's backstory and this vague and mysterious approach makes the monstrous villain much more interesting and enigmatic. This is a lean film without too many pretensions that doesn't take unnecessary detours or waste much time cutting to the chase. The alien has come to Earth to go on safari. He is a hunter. A Predator. The biggest and most challenging prey on Earth as far as the Predators are concerned is man - preferably men who are armed to the teeth.

We open in Guatemala where Major "Dutch" Schaefer (Schwarzenegger) and his elite special forces mercenary team are about to be dropped into a Central American jungle to look for a presidential cabinet minister and aide who were kidnapped by guerrillas in Val Verde after their helicopter crashed. What a team Schwarzenegger has too. They make the Expendables look like puny cub scouts. There is silent killer Mac (the imposing shaven skulled black actor Bill Duke), and the preposterously macho Blain (wrestling star Jesse Ventura) who has a terrifying "M134 minigun" the size of a cannon and says things like "I don't have time to bleed" when he's been shot.

Richard Chaves is "Poncho" Ramirez, their Chicano scout, translator and sharpshooter, and best of all is Sonny Landham (what a fantastic voice) as Native American tracker and jungle expert Billy. Apollo Creed himself Carl Weathers is Dillon, a former colleague of Dutch and now a somewhat mysterious CIA agent. The team are forced to take Dillon with them despite not trusting him at all. Finally, we have Shane Black as Hawkins, the team's bespectacled radio operator and joke dispenser. If Black seems less imposing than most of the others that's because he is. He's primarily a screenwriter and director and had recently written Lethal Weapon and The Monster Squad at the time. Black is not exactly Pee Wee Herman though and looks like he beefed himself up.

Once in the cocooning and steamy tangle of the jungle, the brawny team find the shattered wreckage of the (empty) helicopter and then some skinned bodies hung from trees which they identify as Green Berets from nearby blood stained name tags. This puzzling and grisly sight both mystifies and angers them greatly and they lay waste to a guerilla camp - only sparing a woman named Anna (Elpidia Carrillo) who they take with them.

Dutch begins to realise they have been pawns in a clandestine CIA operation and is eager to get them all to their extraction point and move out of the jungle as soon as possible. But they are of course not alone and their real troubles have only just begun. A formidable and ruthless alien who hunts for sport has been observing them every step of the way from the trees. Armed with heat vision, camouflage technology that makes it invisible, and advanced futuristic weapons, the alien Predator begins to stealthily pick off the team one by one in gruesome fashion as the jungle paranoia increases.

As Anna tells them - "When I was little, we found a man. He looked like - like, butchered. The old woman in the village crossed themselves... and whispered crazy things, strange things. El Diablo cazador de hombres. Only in the hottest years this happens. And this year, it grows hot. We begin finding our men. We found them sometimes without their skins... and sometimes much, much worse. El cazador trofeo de los hombres means the demon who makes trophies of men..." These Predators have clearly been on Earth before. But how you defeat an invisible 7 foot tall alien armed with futuristic weaponry?

Predator is sort of like Rambo meets Alien meets Deliverance meets Southern Comfort. John and Jim Thomas said that Richard Connell's story The Most Dangerous Game was also a big influence on Predator. The Most Dangerous Game follows the story of Sanger Rainsford, a renowned big-game hunter. Rainsford falls off a yacht and swims towards a mysterious island called Ship-Trap Island. He meets General Zaroff, a wealthy Russian aristocrat who has developed an insatiable bloodlust and now hunts humans for sport. John and Jim Thomas said that their concept for 'Hunter', when they first wrote the script, was The Most Dangerous Game crossed with Alien.

The actual Predator alien in the film, though a ruthless killer, is not completely unreasonable and does abide by a code. The Predator only hunts humans who have combat skills and weapons. It would not kill a random unarmed civilian because there would be no sport in that. It wouldn't be a challenge. John McTiernan compared Predator to King Kong in the way that the human characters, so intrepid at the start, have to beat a hasty retreat and run away when they encounter something unexpectedly dangerous! The big twist in Predator is that Dutch and his team, contrary to how the first part of the film sets them up, are shocked to discover they are not - as they had presumed - at the top of the food chain. These invincible Rambos are not invincible in the least when the Predator shows up. The tables are turned - in shocking and grisly fashion.

The derivative (and on the face of it apparently ludicrous) premise and a very troubled production had many predicting that Predator was a disaster in the making. What they didn't know though was that the young unknown director John McTiernan was something of a genius when it came to action films and would make the classic Bruce Willis skyscraper adventure Die Hard the following year. Predator is generally regarded to be something of a cult classic now and the film that established Arnold Schwarzenegger as the world's premier action star at the time - supplanting his great rival Sylvester Stallone.

As the credits roll we see the principle characters emerging from a helicopter one by one in civilian clothes. Schwarzenegger is then shown in silhouette, still in the helicopter and puffing on a huge cigar. He's instantly recognisable and has truly arrived as a cinematic icon. Although Schwarzenegger liked the concept of Predator (the way it began as a traditional action film and then incorporated science fiction and horror elements) he did not want to carry the picture on his own and disliked the simple Schwarzenegger versus alien approach of the original script. So the screenplay became one where Schwarzenegger was part of a team as physically imposing as himself. This was a clever move and the hulking supporting cast are all enjoyable as Predator fodder before Arnie takes centre stage for the third act.

One important element is that we get to know and like the characters before they start to become Predator victims. Therefore we feel a sense of loss when they perish and start to wonder who will be next. Take the Alien vs Predator films by way of comparison. In those films we never feel any connection to the characters and can barely remember who half of them are. The same is true of Shane Black's 2018 sequel The Predator. As a consequence we don't really care when people start dying in those films. In fact we barely notice at all. That isn't the case with the original Predator in the slightest.

The characters in Predator all get memorable deaths too. Take Billy for example. He decides to take on the Predator in unarmed combat on a log bridge merely to buy some time for his friends! Dillon goes down like a hero - even firing on the Predator after having an arm blown off! Predator is always a film that works far better than it has any right to. The lush mist shrouded jungle screens look fantastic and serve as a suitably otherworldly and eerie location for the Predator to go about his bloody business.

If they made Predator today it would probably be a PG-13 with loads of fake looking CGI but here you get people disembowelled, arms severed, chests blown out, people shot, characters constantly swearing. The Predator actually mutilates the bodies of his victims and keeps their skulls as a trophy. The violence is always rather comic book and this is a preposterous film at the best of times but the gore factor definitely makes the picture more memorable and - most importantly - the Predator scarier. Action films today, with their CGI blood splats and green screen CGI backdrops, are just not the same.

The early scenes in the jungle are nicely staged and shot by McTiernan and very Vietnam war film. With the attack on the rebel camp the film becomes Rambo - only bigger and better - and supplies one of the most overblown, ridiculous and enjoyable action sequences in eighties action cinema. Only the climax to Schwarzenegger's Commando where John Matrix took on an entire army with a shotgun and some gardening equipment found in a shed could possibly rival it when it comes to incredibly stupid but somehow brilliant action filmmaking.

It's interesting how the film moves through four distinct acts. When the Predator begins to hunt the team it becomes Ten Little Indians with more than a hint of Southern Comfort. Finally there is a Deliverance/Lord of the Flies back to basics section in the last act. The Predator can't be beaten simply by guns. He has to be outwitted. Beaten at his own game. One thing I like about the film is the way that the characterisations are clear and straight forward. We get a quick sense of who these men are, their history together and how they work as a team. They are a bunch of likeable braggarts to be honest, complacent in the knowledge that they are the absolute best at what they do and more or less indestructible. They joke and banter and the razing of the rebel camp is no problem at all.

But when the Predator begins to pick them off the mood turns serious. They soon realise they are finally out of depth. Some of the dialogue in Predator is a trifle hokey but it's not the sort of film you are supposed to nitpick and it is often hugely quotable. It contains some of Arnie's best one liners ("Stick around!") and does have many memorable flourishes for the actors. "You're ghosting us, mother*****," whispers Bill Duke's Mac to Carl Weathers when Dillon slips on some leaves and makes a noise. "I don't care who you are back in the world, you give away our position one more time, I'll bleed ya, real quiet. Leave ya here. Got that?"

Duke is good value (Mac goes bonkers and develops a personal vendetta against the Predator) and I really like Sonny Landham as the Native American soldier Billy. Billy is imbued with some mystical sixth sense and heightened senses. He is aware they are being watched and followed by something very strange and sinister and whenever he takes on a glazed expression and gazes up at the trees everyone becomes very nervous. The special effects don't always seem state of the art these days but the creature itself still works very well. Most effective are the POV shots we get from the perspective of the Predator. Secretly watching the commando team through his infrared spectrum and mimicking samples of their voices he has recorded (which is very eerie). I like the way they keep the monster in the shadows and then gradually reveal more as the film goes on.

By the way, that creepy clicking noise that indicates a Predator is near or about to strike was based on the noise made by an ailing crab apparently. Weird inspiration but it works. One clever detail in the film is the order of the deaths. The Predator takes out the team's radio operator first to complicate their communications. It then takes out Blain - who is equipped with the team's deadliest weapon. Not only that but it takes out Blain from long distance so that he won't have any chance to use his weapon.

Maybe the Predator seems a bit lumbering at times but it's fun the way it leaps from trees and matches wits with the commando team. We establish too that the Predator does have a basic hunting code and set of ethics. He spares Anna when he could easily kill her because she has no weapon and therefore is no sport. The rest won't be so lucky. You could argue that Predator is the best acting performance of Arnold Schwarzenegger's career. Dutch is a believable charismatic leader of these men but he's also very human. Dutch is genuinely terrified at times in this film and him and his men actually try to run away from the Predator in the end.

Despite his muscles and military exploits, Dutch is actually one of the more vulnerable characters Arnie played in his action movie prime. You never saw John Matrix in Commando look scared or find himself out of his depth in the way that Dutch does. The supporting performances are very good too - especially Carl Weathers as Dillon. The film avoids cliches too by not having a traitor or human villain among the characters. Dillon is the closest we get but he redeems himself in the end and turns out to be brave and have a moral compass. John McTiernan said he cast Carl Weathers because because Schwarzenegger wasn't a very experienced actor at the time and wanted a good solid actor alongside Arnold.

Predator is a hugely enjoyable slab of eighties action fun and classic Arnie. It has a great monster and is wonderfully co-ordinated by John McTiernan. Perhaps the best thing about the film is that it retains a strange ability to hold your attention again no matter how many times you've seen it before. Oh, and this has the best men shooting guns at nothing sequence in cinematic history. They must have destroyed half the rainforest before they realised the Predator had done a bunk!

Predator frequently crops up now on 'best of' lists when it comes to action and horror films. From a modern vantage point it isn't hard to see why the film's reputation has grown steadily over the decades. We live in an age today where the most of the blockbuster films are loud, shallow, and frequently annoying. Giant robots fighting each other, superhero movies that all blur into one in the end, CGI cities being destroyed. By contrast Predator is a model of restraint and economy. It slowly builds tension and atmosphere and the last act is not bombastic and full of explosions but more intimate and stripped down. Dutch has to become primitive to defeat the alien. He has to use wits rather than guns.

One could argue that Predator has a lot of subtext for an action film. The subtext of Predator is that guns can't solve all problems. Dutch and his men prove to be (ahem) expendable as far as the authorities are concerned. They are men out of time working for people who have questionable ethics. As great as Arnold is, the real star of the film is the Predator itself. This was a great movie monster who we definitely wanted to see more of. Predator actually got some sniffy and snooty reviews from critics when it first came out but there were plenty of good ones too and the reputation of the film has grown over the years.

Predator is now considered to be a classic of eighties action cinema and something of a unique experience in the way that it walks a tightrope between action, horror, and science fiction and yet does each of these difference facets exceptionally well. Somewhat overlooked too is how incredibly downbeat the ending of Predator is. Dutch has vanquished the Predator and survived but he's clearly a broken and lonely man at the end. All of his friends and comrades are dead. Predator had the second biggest opening weekend gross of any film in 1987. It ended up grossing around $100 million - which was a more than decent haul considering its fairly modest budget. This meant that a sequel was all but assured. The Predator was such a great movie monster that it simply had to come back. Soon there would be Predator comics and Predator computer games. A new franchise had been born.

PREDATOR 2 (1990)

Predator was a surprising success story after all the production difficulties and looked set to become the next big 20th Century Fox franchise. A sequel was soon on the drawing board but hit a number of obstacles before it had even begun production. A hesitant Arnold Schwarzenegger disliked the central premise (the Predator hunts in an urban city setting instead of a jungle) and became unavailable anyway due to the production of James Cameron's Terminator 2: Judgment Day being pushed forward. There was no chance of Arnold not doing Terminator 2. The Terminator franchise was very dear to his heart and James Cameron was a good friend. Schwarzenegger also knew that Terminator 2 was most likely going to be the biggest film of his career.

Though he did return many years later to do some voice work for a Predator video game, it seems that Schwarzenegger never had any particular love for the Predator franchise - certainly in comparison to Terminator and Conan. Appearing in Predator 2 was evidently something that didn't interest him very much. It could be the case that Arnold simply wanted to move on and do other things. He was signed up for Total Recall and Terminator 2 soon after Predator so one can probably understand his situation. He wanted to work with Paul Verhoeven (red hot at the time after Robocop) and also James Cameron again. Arnold also made the comedy films Twins and Kindergarten Cop around this time. He was clearly seeking to branch out from his violent action roles and do some family films.

Strange though it might have seemed at the time, we would never see Arnold reprise his role as Dutch in a Predator film again. Maybe though that wasn't necessarily such a bad thing because it meant the Predator franchise became an anthology in that each film featured completely new characters going up against the Predator. That would help keep things fresh. Still, the departure of Arnold was definitely a concern for the studio because he was such a big star. There is no question that the absence of Schwarzenegger in Predator 2 did the box-office gross no favours. How do you replace Arnold Schwarzenegger circa 1989? You can't really. The only actors near his stature (bankability, fame etc) at that specific time in Hollywood were Mel Gibson, Harrison Ford and maybe Kevin Costner and none of them were going to appear in Predator 2. The same went for Bruce Willis and Sly Stallone.

To make matters even worse, John McTiernan, now one of the hottest directors in Hollywood after Predator and Die Hard, also declined to return for Predator 2 because he chose instead to direct The Hunt For Red October with Sean Connery. Predator 2 would now have to go ahead without both McTiernan and Schwarzenegger and these were obviously two very big pairs of shoes to fill. They were impossible shoes to fill if you were being honest. Short of hiring James Cameron or Paul Verhoeven (neither of whom were realistic options or available anyway) to direct Predator 2, anyone was going to be a downgrade after McTiernan.

Jim and John Thomas, who wrote the first film, supplied some story ideas to Fox for a Predator sequel as part of their contract. They came up with a number of different ideas. One of these had the Predators investigating the events of the first film and seeking to hunt down Dutch. Another idea was that the film would take place in a snowy forest during the Battle of the Bulge - with the Predator hunting both German and Allied soldiers. The Ardennes Offensive (Unternehmen Wacht am Rhein - Operation Watch on the Rhine) was Hitler's last desperate gamble in the Western theatre of World War 2. On December the 16th, 1944, he launched the offensive - destined to become equally well known as 'The Battle of the Bulge' because of the 'bulge' it created in the Allied front line positions. It was an audacious but impossible gambit that squandered Germany's last coherent armoured reserves in the West and probably hastened the end of the war.

One of the concepts by Jim and John Thomas for a sequel had the Predator hunting in present day New York. The studio liked this concept because it would make the sequel feel different from the first film and not merely an imitation. It probably isn't a coincidence that the Predator comics by Dark Horse began at this time and featured the Predator in a big city. The makers of Predator 2 actually had some meetings with the Predator comic book people to make sure their concepts didn't clash too much. When they were throwing ideas around for Predator 2, Jim and John Thomas also thought about doing a steampunk Predator story with the alien hunting in the Old West or something like that. Nothing came of this at the time but we finally got a period Predator film decades later with Prey.

The original story concept for what became Predator 2 was that Dutch would team up with a big city cop named Harrigan to battle a Predator. At first they clash but then work together. Basically then, the concept behind Predator 2 was to do it as a 'buddy cop action movie' - only with the Predator as the villain. It is often reported that Gary Busey's mysterious special agent was the part earmarked for Schwarzenegger - with the plan being that Dutch from the first film was going to be part of some special task force hunting the alien in sequels. However, this is apparently not completely accurate and the plan was for BOTH Dutch and Keyes to be in the film.

When it became clear that Arnold Schwarzenegger was not available, the character of Harrigan became the main lead and the role of Keyes was expanded. They basically had to rejig the script to adapt to the fact that Dutch wasn't going to be in it. The producer John Davis said the reason that Schwarzenegger didn't do Predator 2 is because of money. Davis claims that Arnold wanted $250,000 more than they were willing to pay him so walked away from the sequel. This tends to clash with other explanations of why Arnold didn't return. If true though it seems rather odd that the studio were not willing to pay a bit more to secure the services of one of Hollywood's biggest stars. Schwarzenegger's name on the Predator 2 poster would have added some welcome extra revenue.

The person chosen to direct Predator 2 in the end was Stephen Hopkins. Hopkins was only 29 years-old. The only thing of note Hopkins had directed at the time was one of the many Nightmare On Elm Street sequels but he would later become best known (and most respected) for his producing and directing duties on the Kiefer Sutherland action series 24. Hopkins had directed a 1987 Australian thriller called Dangerous Game - which in turn got him the job of directing A Nightmare on Elm Street 5: The Dream Child. Hopkins was an interesting and cosmopolitan character. He was born in Jamaica and spent part of his youth in both England and Australia. 20th Century Fox were clearly hoping that by hiring a young, energetic up and coming director they might able to repeat what happened when the young, energetic and largely unknown James Cameron was chosen to direct Aliens.

Stephen Hopkins said that when he got the job of directing Predator 2 he still hadn't actually seen the first movie so he watched it multiple times to get an understanding of the Predator character and what sort of franchise he was walking into. Hopkins actually consulted with John McTiernan and said McTiernan was generous and kind enough to offer some advice. The script wasn't completed when Hopkins was hired so he was able to have some input into the story.

Hopkins said he did have a meeting with Arnold Schwarzenegger about Predator 2 but nothing came of this. He said Arnold was very polite and courteous but was simply unavailable with Terminator 2 looming. "Terminator 2: Judgment Day was going to happen at around the same time," said Hopkins, "and Jim Cameron said to Arnold: Do one or the other – don't do both. It's hard to turn down one of the greatest science fiction films ever made. I was quite close to shooting and Arnold suddenly disappeared from the project."

This obviously meant that Mike Harrigan would now be the big leading character taking on the Predator. The first choice for the part of Harrigan was Patrick Swayze. Swayze was a big star at the time thanks to Dirty Dancing (and had an even bigger hit in 1990 with Ghost). Patrick Swayze had to drop out of contention though after he got injured making the film Road House. Swayze was an interesting and very plausible choice because he was a very competent actor and also no stranger to action movies. Alas though it wasn't to be. Stephen Hopkins later said he didn't have any dealings with Patrick Swayze or know much about this potential casting what might have been. It evidently happened before Hopkins joined the film.

Stephen Hopkins said he did though have to resist studio pressure trying to persuade him to cast none other than Steven Seagal as the lead in Predator 2. Seagal was still relatively new in Hollywood at the time but had quickly established himself as the new action star on the block with 1988's Above the Law. Seagal had a raft of movies in the pipeline (Marked for Death and Hard to Kill both came out in 1990 - the same year as the Predator sequel) but was still very eager to be in Predator 2. Stephen Hopkins was not so keen though. He thought that having Seagal as the lead in Predator 2 was a terrible idea and one to be avoided at all costs.

Hopkins had a meeting with Seagal - which he said was rather eccentric (Seagal offered to take Hopkins to his ranch to show him his rocket launcher!) and wasn't too impressed with Seagal's pitch. Seagal wanted his character in Predator 2 to be a mystical CIA agent who - of course - is also an aikido master. It's hard to imagine that aikido would be of much use against a Predator! Hopkins definitely didn't want Seagal as the star of Predator 2 and managed to block this casting. Hopkins, one suspects, feared that Predator 2 would simply have come off as a Steven Seagal film - which is something he didn't want at all.

What would happened though if the studio had got their way and Steven Seagal was the star of Predator 2? Would it have worked? It's hard to see how having Seagal as the star of Predator 2 would have been an improvement over what we got. Seagal was very popular in his day and good at fight scenes but he wasn't much of an actor and tends to just give the same performance in every single film. A big part of the Predator franchise too is that the hero is usually completely out of their depth against the Predator and has to take a lot of punishment. Steven Seagal never takes any punishment in his films. You never see one of his characters taking a pounding.

Also, would Steven Seagal have been willing to play a character who is believably terrified of this monstrous alien in the way that even Arnold did in the first film? Seagal is not an actor who conveys any emotion at all - least of all fear! While the thought of Steven Seagal going up against the Predator has guilty pleasure written all over it, in the end sanity prevailed and the studio agreed with Hopkins that Predator 2 needed a leading man who was at least an experienced actor.

In the end it was Danny Glover who signed to play Harrigan. Glover was a fine actor who had two Emmy award nominations and had also appeared in films like Witness, Silverado, and the Lethal Weapon series. Some people at the time assumed Glover was a bit old and portly for the lead action role in Predator 2 but they were wrong. What they didn't realise was that (in a rarity for Hollywood) in the Lethal Weapon movies Glover was aged up somewhat and played a character ten years older than his actual age. Around the time of Predator 2, Danny Glover was still in his early forties and did a lot of running and weight lifting to prepare for playing Harrigan. He got into fantastic shape for the film.

Danny Glover is physically imposing in Predator 2 and believable as a tough police officer who takes no nonsense from anyone - not even his boss! He is also a very good actor and so gives the film an anchor of credibility that it wouldn't have had if Steven Seagal had played the lead. Mike Harrigan is a badass and Danny

Glover takes the credit for that. The studio wanted John Lithgow for the part of Peter Keyes but this obviously didn't transpire. In the end it was Gary Busey who bagged this part. Busey was already a veteran actor with a long CV. It is no coincidence that Busey, like Glover, was in Lethal Weapon because Joel Silver produced both Lethal Weapon and Predator 2.

Joel Silver was actually in the 20th Century Fox doghouse during Predator 2 because Die Hard 2 was going over budget and Silver got the blame. Stephen Hopkins said that the studio banned Silver from the Predator 2 set as a consequence. Gary Busey had been in a bad motorcycle accident in 1988 in which he suffered a fractured skull and brain damage. Predator 2 was his first comeback film since the accident. Stephen Hopkins said that Busey could be a bit loud and hyper and he had to tell him to tone down his performance as Keyes a few times. It obviously wouldn't be a very balanced performance if Keyes was constantly shouting all the time!

A fairly strong supporting cast was put in place for Predator 2 with Maria Conchita Alonso, Ruben Blades, and Bill Paxton cast as police officers. Blades had been in films like The Milagro Beanfield War and had a busy time around Predator 2 because he was also in The Two Jakes and the Spike Lee film Mo' Better Blues. María Conchita Alonso is a Cuban singer, actress and former beauty queen. She had many credits and a few years earlier was in The Running Man with Arnold Schwarzenegger.

Bill Paxton obviously needs no introduction. His role as Hudson in Aliens had instantly made him a cult actor. His other credits included Near Dark, The Terminator, and Weird Science. Robert Davi, who had just played a Bond villain in Licence To Kill, was cast the police chief who clashes with Harrigan and Kevin Peter Hall was once again in the Predator suit. Sadly, Hall passed away in 1991 - not long after the film came out.

Elpidia Carrillo was supposed to have a cameo as Anna in Predator 2. Keyes was going show Harrigan some video footage of

Anna discussing the Predator. Though this scene was shot it was cut from the movie so all you see now is a still of Anna on a screen. Lilyan Chauvin, who plays Dr Irene Edwards, was a French actress with credits stretching back to the 1950s. Kent McCord, who plays Captain Brent Pilgrim, was a film and TV veteran who once appeared in a film with Elvis. Eighties kids might remember McCord from Galactica 1980 - which was a short lived spin-off from Battlestar Galactica.

Adam Baldwin plays Agent Adam Garber in Predator 2. Adam Baldwin is NOT related to Alec Baldwin or a member of the Baldwin clan - though it is easy to make this mistake. Adam Baldwin had a small role in Stanley Kubrick's Full Metal Jacket and later did a lot of television work. You may have seen him in things like Firefly and Castle. The weirdest piece of casting is Morton Downey Jr as Tony Pope, a journalist for some trashy news channel who reports on the Predator murders. Morton Downey Jr was a real life larger than life talk show host - he was sort of Jerry Springer before Jerry Springer.

The Predator in this sequel was given different patterns and made to look sleeker than the creature in the first film because they wanted it to be clear that this is a completely different Predator (the Predator in the first film obviously blew itself up after being defeated by Dutch). One big change which occurred before shooting began is that the story now took place in Los Angeles rather than New York. This decision was made to save money because shooting in Los Angeles was a lot more convenient than shooting in New York or making Los Angeles look like New York. Alan Silvestri returned to score the movie. Predator 2 had a budget of between $20 and $30 million - which was more than the first film.

Predator 2 began shooting in February 1990 and wrapped in June 1990. A lot of scenes were shot in downtown Los Angeles - which was a dangerous place at the time. Stephen Hopkins said they hired street gang members to protect the crew. Hopkins said the crew members got shot at a few times. There were a lot of homeless people in the shooting locations at night. The big sequence where the government military team try to catch the Predator in the frosty slaughterhouse was a nightmare to shoot and took four weeks to complete. It was shot in a warehouse and everyone had to wear masks for real because of all the dust.

The subway sequence in Predator 2 was inspired by the Alien vs Predator comics. The subway scenes were shot on a soundstage in Los Angeles and then additional scenes with moving trains were shot in Oakland, California. The cemetery scene was filmed at the Angelus Rosedale Cemetery on West Washington Way. The scene were the Predator scales a lightning crackled building was shot at the Art Deco Eastern Columbia Building at 849 South Broadway. The rooftop scene near the start of the film was shot at 604 South Main Street in LA. The climax was shot at Belmont Tunnel, 1304 W 2nd St, Los Angeles.

Harrigan's sidearm in Predator 2 is a brushed chrome .357 Magnum chambered Desert Eagle Mark VII. The laser sight was added to give the weapon a more futuristic look. Predator 2 was the first film to be given the newly instituted NC-17 rating in the United States. A lot of cuts had to be made to bring the rating down. Stephen Hopkins said his approach to the movie was to go over the top and have fun and this included plenty of gore. The Jamaican gang using voodoo in the film is not actually accurate. Voodoo comes from Haiti - not Jamaica. If the first film takes its cue from films like Deliverance and Southern Comfort, Predator 2 is inspired by urban cop thrillers. The alien in this sequel is not going after military men this time but police officers and criminals. Could the sequel live up to the original? Well, let's discuss the film and find out.

REVIEW

It's the far off future year of 1997 and Los Angeles is an overcrowded simmering heat hazed powder keg being torn apart by a violent war between dangerous Colombian and Jamaican drug cartels. At the start of the film Detective Harrigan (Danny Glover) intervenes in a dangerous shoot out between the warring factions on the street as a new Predator watches from afar - doubtless impressed by what he has seen. The Colombians are driven back to their headquarters but the Predator has already been there when Harrigan and fellow detectives Leona Cantrell (Maria Conchita Alonso) and Danny Archuleta (Ruben Blades) enter the building. Bodies are skinned and strung from the ceiling in the usual Predator fashion and suspicion turns to the Jamaicans and their allegiance to black magic rituals.

But the Jamaicans start to be killed too in equally gruesome fashion. A third party is clearly involved. Someone who obviously knows more than he is letting on is Special Agent Peter Keyes (Gary Busey), the leader of a federal task force apparently investigating the cartels. The secretive Keyes - who always arrives on the scene with his men in black - tells Harrigan and his team to keep their nose out of this affair but things are about to get very personal and the detective is soon more embroiled than anyone in this puzzling and dangerous case...

Predator 2, with no Arnold Schwarzenegger to stick on the top of the poster, always seemed destined to be the strange sequel that no one even remembers but this is a slick and underrated film with a B-movie exploitation charm that piles on the Predator mayhem and gore in gleeful fashion. Happily, Predator 2 now seems to be mildly cultish and much more appreciated these days than it was at the time. The film, if we discount the AvP movies, is still though the lowest rated Predator film on Rotten Tomatoes.

I can't say I agree with that consensus at all. In fact, I find Predator 2 to be almost as rewatchable as the first film (though obviously not in the same league) and always have a good time whenever I watch it again. For my money at least, Predator 2 is more entertaining than Predators and The Predator so I certainly can't agree with its lowly rating. Predator 2 does fare better on IMDB user reviews. It ranks above The Predator on IMDB and has more or less the same ranking as Predators.

Predator 2 seems rather small scale and unambitious at times (and unavoidably more generic than the first picture with the urban setting) but if you can park your brain at the door and accept it for what it is then Predator 2 is very enjoyable undemanding nonsense and much better than its reputation would suggest. And the film does the Predator character justice too. I'd argue that the Predator carnage in this film is highly inventive and very entertaining. The alien is spoilt for choice when it comes to targets in this sequel and slaughters people by the dozen.

The casting is rather eccentric and scattershot here but sort of works. Danny Glover is a commanding presence as the lead and adds a splash of humanity to the part of Harrigan. Glover makes a surprisingly great action hero in Predator 2 and he also supplies some gravitas. Although the film lacks a big headline star and the larger than life Expendables style supporting cast of the original Predator there are a host of familiar names here. Bill Paxton is Detective Jerry Lambert, another member of Harrigan's team and essays another over the top wisecracking Bill Paxton turn while Calvin Lockhart (forever enshrined in my memory as the wooden and wonderfully theatrical big game hunter in The Beast Must Die) is King Willie, the boss of the Jamaica Voodoo Posse.

Stephen Hopkins overdoes the voodoo drug baron capers a bit but it adds some atmosphere to the picture and gives the Predator plenty of people to kill. Ethnic drug gangs as villains and cannon fodder were all the rage in action films of this era and this aspect is obviously rather dated from a modern vantage point. Predator 2 is very much a product of its time. That's a great scene where King Willie takes on the Predator in an alley and his screams are cut into a shot of the Predator walking away with his head. It's a shame though that the Predator's legs look a trifle on the fake and rubbery side!

Gary Busey chews the scenery up as Keyes and while I don't think there will ever be an Oscar sitting on the Busey mantlepiece he's sort of fun (with his hubristic attitude we just know he is heading for a downfall) and has a pivotal role in what is the most memorable set-piece in the film. This is highly derivative of a sequence in James Cameron's Aliens where the space marines go into action watched on small video monitors but terrific nonetheless. Keyes and his team track the Predator down to a huge meat warehouse fridge (where the Predator goes to feed) and enter with cryogenic weapons and foam suits to negate its infrared thermal vision.

They plan to freeze and capture the extraterrestrial rascal. Good plan but as you can imagine though the Predator is much craftier than they've given him credit for and much carnage ensues. That's a great moment when the Predator begins to suspect something is afoot and adjusts its sight technology to decipher Keyes and his men in the gloom. This set-piece is one of my favourite sequences in any Predator film.

The other excellent set-piece in the film has the Predator on a subway train where it's up to Detectives Lambert and Cantrell to somehow hold him off so passengers can get to safety. Lot of screaming and lights going on and off. The city doesn't work as well as the jungle as a location but there is some great stuff here nonetheless. The sequence where Lambert is trapped by the Predator on the train is genuinely terrifying. "Want some candy?" Never has a line in the Predator franchise been so strange and frightening!

What doesn't work so well in Predator 2 is the occasional lapse into slapstick in the third act when the Predator crashes into the apartment of a couple of pensioners like Inspector Closeau. This lurch into a more comedic tone seems out of character for what is often an incredibly violent and gruesome film (for a mainstream Hollywood release).

There are a few tonal lurches in Predator 2 like this that the movie could probably have done without. In mitigation though, Stephen Hopkins has obviously gone for a kitchen sink approach to Predator 2 and - when you weigh things up on average - more stuff lands than misses.

You are never too far away from some violence or action in Predator 2 and that's fine because it gives you something different from the first picture. The worst thing they could have done in Predator 2 is stick a new bunch of characters in a jungle and tried to repeat the first film. Predator 2 is at least its own thing by dint of having an urban location and a different director. The sequences where the Predator kills the drug barons and their assorted goons in penthouses are enjoyably blood drenched and move the film firmly into horror territory. The Predator has some nifty gadgets in this one. A frisbee, razor sharp nets, a huge spear thing that can retract or expand (very nasty).

My favourite scene in Predator 2 is when Harrigan barely escapes after the Predator has killed many people in a confined area. Detective Harrigan takes to a rooftop and constantly looks over his shoulder and around each corner with great trepidation as the camera swings around to give us his point of view. He's believably terrified and this short sequence is as tense as anything in the first film. One weakness though is the juvenile MTV aura that permeates the film at times. Loud music and gratuitous nudity. The actual detective investigation into the Predator is a little wearing at times too. We (the audience) obviously already know the culprit behind all the murders is an alien hunter from outer space.

It helps that Alan Silvestri again supplies the score and Stan Winston does sterling work again. His idea was that maybe this Predator was younger and more impulsive. Sleeker and faster. He certainly has more fangs. That jarring electronic noise when we see from the Predator point of view in infrared is still scary. Morton Downey Jr as Tony Pope, doesn't work. "This is Tony Pope, live from L.A, the city of fear. Where the psycho vigilante killer continues his daily diet for murder. Bodies strung out. Bodies with the skins ripped off. The hearts torn from the cadavers. And just recently, King Willie, the drug lord. The vicious drug lord, found in an alley just around the corner with his head cut off, and his spinal column torn from the body. A fitting demise to the Prince of Powder."

This stuff feels like a vague attempt to inject some Robocop style satire into the film but Morton Downey Jr (a real life talk show host playing a thinly veiled version of himself) soon becomes annoying. It's fun at the end to go onboard a Predator ship and Danny Glover earns his place in the gallery of Predator franchise badasses when he declares "Who's next?" after a group of Predators surround him. By the way, it's nice to see that the Predator code of honour, that sense of fair play, is present here. The Predator in this film refuses to hurt a child and a pregnant woman and the Predators at the end let Harrigan live. He is tossed an antique pistol - which obviously indicates these alien hunters have been coming to Earth for a long time.

And yes, that's a xenomorph skull in the Predator ship. For better or for worse (and in this case it was definitely for worse) an Alien versus Predator film was inevitable. It was bound to happen one day. The MTV aura of Predator 2 is explained not just by the era it was made (you could say that Predator 2 is more or less a 1980s film) but also because Stephen Hopkins began his career directing music videos. Hopkins was also a comic book artist - which would explain why Predator 2 is the most comic book Predator film. There is less substance to Predator 2 than the first film. Hopkins is a flashier and more disposable director than John McTiernan - he simply isn't as good.

However, Hopkins knows how to blow things up and give you an entertaining show. He gives us some inventive Predator kills and some great action set-pieces. Hopkins said that on Predator 2 he was just a young director having fun and that comes through in the film. Predator 2 is fun. It isn't meant to be taken too seriously. Despite the dismal reviews that surrounded Predator 2 and the fact that it has been largely forgotten by many in the decades since its release, this is a very underrated sequel.

If you can accept the fact there is no Schwarzenegger and that this is a different beast (no pun intended) then you should get a lot of fun out of Predator 2. Cartoonish direction, a frenetic pace, lashings of gore, some vivid set-pieces, and even a decent ending. Hardly subtle and not nearly as iconic as the first film but Predator 2 is brash, bold, entertaining and does what it says on the box. And few films have surely had such a great tagline - "Silent. Invisible. Invincible. He's in town with a few days to kill."

Sadly, Predator 2 got dreadful reviews. The critics seemed to save all their snootiest disdain for this film. Most critics seemed to find the film mean spirited and too violent. The most bizarre review came from the late Roger Ebert - who said the film was racist because the Predator's dreadlocks were designed to connect it to a racist fear of black males. This was a rather strange point to make about a film in which the hero is black. Presumably then, according to Roger Ebert, Stan Winston must have been a racist because he designed the Predator in the first place.

Predator 2 was also a box-office disappointment. It grossed $57 million - which was considerably less than the first film. It seems that, for whatever reason, few people ever really gave Predator 2 much of a chance. It seems to plausible to think that the film was hobbled by the fact that Arnold Schwarzenegger didn't return. Taken on its own terms though, Predator 2 is a blast. Sure, it's a bit goofy and hokey in places but it has some great action sequences and the Predator antics are enjoyably gruesome and well up to par.

The film is also, with the city setting and new slate of characters, different enough from the first film not to feel like a pale rehash. The failure of Predator 2 to find an audience obviously meant that no one was in a rush to make Predator 3. Story ideas were thrown around but nothing went into production. In fact, we would have to wait 20 years for the next stand alone Predator film to come out. In the meantime we got the Alien versus Predator movies.

ALIEN VS PREDATOR (2004)

Alien vs Predator was a Dark Horse comic series that dated back as far as the late eighties. The Alien and Predator film franchises may have petered out sooner than expected but the memorable creations of HR Giger and Stan Winston got a new lease of life in comics when someone had the clever idea of pitting them against one another in the most anticipated monster smackdown since King Kong fought Godzilla. But while this concept had worked in comics could it work in a film? Comics and films are not the same thing (just ask Alan Moore). A film version of the AvP comics had long been mused on by the studio and 1990's Predator 2 famously featured a xenomorph skull in the Predator's trophy room.

A British screenwriter named Peter Briggs sold an Alien vs Predator script in 1991 to Fox but it was never put into production. "I wrote that first draft in a 6 week period in 1991," said Briggs, "basically to get out of a development grind at Paramount UK that was driving me nuts, in the desperate hope that I could use it as a sample to land a rewrite gig with someone like Joel Silver. Weirdly, I sold it overnight instead to 20th Century Fox, and it set the project along its tortured path. If Joe Roth had stayed at Fox, we could have been spared Alien Resurrection, and my draft might have happened. Though it would have cost a whole helluva lot more to make than Paul Anderson's....er, tale. Probably a 100 mill. At least 60-80." *

The script by Briggs was called The Hunt: Alien vs Predator and was clearly inspired by the Dark Horse comics. The story had the Predators seeding planets with xenomorph eggs so they can go there to hunt aliens. The jungle planet Ryushi becomes a battleground between Predators, xenomorphs, and the unfortunate human colonists who happen to live there.

Alien producer David Giler was opposed to an Alien vs Predator film and Sigourney Weaver disliked the concept too. They both felt it would only further dilute the Alien franchise. Weaver claimed that she only made Alien 3 to nix an Alien v Predator film and was generally dismissive of the concept.

Alien vs Predator was sort of like Fox's plan B in the event of the two franchises hitting a dead end. That time had finally arrived. The Predator franchise had been mothballed since since the tepid reaction to Predator 2 and Alien Resurrection seemed to be the final nail in the coffin of the Alien franchise. Alien Resurrection is generally considered to be the worst of the four Alien films - and by some considerable distance. There is something completely off about Alien Resurrection to the point where it never quite feels like an Alien film. Alien Resurrection is too comic book and goofy. It feels cartoonish.

The characters in the first three Alien films felt like real people going about their business in the midst of the story. Even the characters in the more popcorn action heavy Aliens felt authentic and served the story. The characters in Alien Resurrection feel cardboard and fake. The actors are often reduced to posing in their ridiculous space pirate costumes as they spew out quips and some terrible dialogue. Alien Resurrection is a bizarre coda to the Sigourney Weaver Alien movies. Parts of the film are entertaining, parts of the film are silly, parts of the film are harrowing, parts of the film are stupid. Whatever way you slice it up, the main problem with Alien Resurrection is that the director doesn't appear to be taking the film seriously.

Alien Resurrection is the closest the Alien franchise ever came to making a black comedy. Alien Resurrection gives you more bang for your buck than the Alien 3 but it still somehow ends up being the least satisfying of the four films. Alien Resurrection got mixed reviews from critics (current RT consensus - 55%) and was a relative failure at the North American box-office (although like previous Alien films it did better overseas). Fans of the franchise were - generally - not happy at the film's somewhat goofy comic book tone.

The 2004 Alien vs Predator movie is said to have ruined a chance of James Cameron and Ridley Scott returning to make a new Alien film together. Very depressing if true! "To me, that was Frankenstein Meets Werewolf," said Cameron of the AvP concept. "It was Universal just taking their assets and starting to play them off against each other. Milking it." Strangely though, Cameron later said he enjoyed Alien vs Predator and ranked it as the third best Alien film after the first two (which is damning with faint praise - and Cameron has every reason to dislike Alien 3 given that it bumped off Hicks and Newt so meanly and casually).

That was always the problem with the Alien series. It lost its way after the classic first two pictures. No one could ever live up to the standards set by Alien and Aliens. Alien 3, thanks mostly to the assembly cut (a longer version of the film later released on DVD), certainly has its fans but it was hugely divisive and incredibly grim. It was probably inevitable that Fox would turn back to the Alien vs Predator concept once the Alien series fizzled out. From their point of view it was a new way to make more money out of an IP that had hit a dead end.

In the early nineties Roland Emmerich was asked to direct an Alien vs Predator film but it never happened in the end. It is said that Arnold Schwarzenegger would have been asked to reprise his Predator character Dutch in the film. Given that Schwarzenegger was the biggest box-office star in the world at the dawn of the nineties and turned down Predator 2, it's hard to think he would have been interested in Alien vs Predator at the time. Arnold actually went on record in 2015 to say that he didn't like any of the Predator sequels. Arnold's disdain for sequels though didn't stop him from appearing in two dreadful Terminator films (Genisys and Dark Fate).

Guillermo Del Toro was later offered the chance to direct the first Alien vs Predator but turned it down because he was busy developing Hellboy. The film only gained traction when producer John Davis had a meeting with Resident Evil director Paul W. S Anderson and liked his pitch for a proposed Alien vs Predator film. "Alien vs Predator had a torturous history," said Anderson.

"Fox have had a script for it for ten years, ever since Peter Briggs did an adaption of the comic book. And yet they didn't make it; Alien still had an active franchise and the producers not seeing eye to eye was a stumbling block.

"I think a lot of them don't actually get on. But by the time I was involved, there was a sense at the studio that they were dead franchises. The last two Alien movies and the last Predator movie were severe disappointments, financially. I went to see Predator producer John Davis and I pitched the idea I'd been kind of working out in my mind for the last 10 years. John said, "I've heard 150, 200, 250 pitches on AVP, had a dozen scripts done, but this is the best idea I've ever heard!' We went to Fox three days later and within a month I was writing the script."

Paul W. S Anderson had actually been in contention to direct Alien Resurrection in the mid nineties. Anderson is said to have got as far as discussions with studio brass but scheduling complications eventually removed him from the frame. "It's got what you want from an Alien movie; guns and lots of Aliens running around," said Anderson in a 1997 interview. "In a way, it would have been a great movie to do because I love Alien movies. But I've grown up with Alien. I saw 20 years ago what the Alien could do and it still does the same thing. I think that's the problem with a lot of monster movies - how do you scare people with it?"

It would probably be fair to say that Paul W. S. Anderson was not exactly a respected A-List director. He made his debut with the low-budget British film Shopping but thereafter his stock in trade became slick but low-budget and shallow sci-fi actioners - usually based on video games. His films based on Resident Evil and Mortal Kombat both drew bad reviews and his film Soldier didn't fare much better. His sci-fi horror film Event Horizon didn't get very good reviews either - though it is generally still considered to be his best film since Shopping. **

"AVP is not trying to be Alien or Aliens," Anderson told the BBC, "and it's not trying to be Predator. Those are genius movies. The impact that these creatures had on audiences was immense. But 26 years on, and dozens of comicbooks later, everyone knows what the Alien looks like. You've got to do something different with it, and make a slightly different movie. So in a way we were definitely making an Alien and a Predator movie, but a different one from the one the other directors had made."

Anderson's story for Alien vs Predator was inspired by Erich von Däniken (the Swiss author famous for his theories on how alien visitors influenced ancient civilisations on Earth) and Lovecraft's At the Mountains of Madness. At the Mountains of Madness is one of Lovecraft's most famous and enduring stories and remains hugely influential. The story is set in the lonely windswept interior of the Antarctic plateau and told by Professor William Dyer - a geologist from Miskatonic University. Dyer's terrible tale is a warning to a planned scientific expedition of Antarctica not to travel to this frozen outpost and follow in his footsteps. He led a team of scholars from Miskatonic University there to extract geological and biological specimens but what they found was so horrifying that his official report had to be censored.

Ancient pre-human alien life forms, a lost city, biological engineers who dissect humans for experimentation, creatures so indescribably hideous that one look at them would lead to insanity, and giant penguins. Generally, Lovecraft's pantheon of Elder Things and his rather bleak take on the universe. A vast random indifferent place without any spiritual meaning where man is inconsequential. Dyer and his team have barely hit the ice when their dogs start to act strangely and bark all the time. Strange blob creatures millions of years old are found in a cave and this will merely be the tip of the (ahem) iceberg. "I could not help feeling that they were evil things - mountains of madness whose farther slopes looked out over some accursed ultimate abyss..."

The pyramid in Anderson's Alien vs Predator film is a concept from the original Alien that was never used so Dan O'Bannon (who wrote the original script on which Alien was based) was given a story credit. The early concept for Alien was that the characters would find a strange pyramid on the nightmare planet but this was obviously dropped in the end. O'Bannon said that Paul W. S Anderson didn't though use his suggestion that the Predators were really the xenomorphs in a further stage of evolution!

Anderson was told by the studio not to set the film in space or an alien world and so chose a subantarctic location in present day Earth. Cynics could suggest that they set the film on present day Earth to save money. It seems that 20th Century Fox were somewhat circumspect in their approach to Alien vs Predator. The budget was modest and no big names were hired - either behind the camera or in front of it. The studio approach to Alien vs Predator was what you might describe as half-hearted.

Paul W. S Anderson said he didn't want to threaten the continuity of the Alien series and so the events of his film had to be isolated and out of the way. "The movie is very much designed as a prequel to Alien and feeds into that story," said Anderson. "When the Nostromo diverts itself to check out the derelict, it is clear Weyland knows about the existence of those aliens. They are not discovering them for the first time. This movie explains how that first piece of information falls into their hands."

The first actor cast in the film was the ever reliable and ever available Lance Henriksen. Henriksen (appearing in his third Alien film if you want to include Alien vs Predator) was to play Charles Bishop Weyland - a wealthy businessman who was clearly the inspiration for the android Bishop and the billionaire head of Weyland Industries, a subsidiary of the Weyland Corporation, which he is also the head of. "I was the first one cast in the movie," said Henriksen. "Paul and I met in the Beverly Hills Hotel; we sat around having coffee and Paul was gracious enough to literally for two hours tell me every scene in the movie. I was stunned because he has this incredible enthusiasm for what he's doing and what his vision is that he had energy to do that. So I was really welcomed. It wasn't like a bunch of strangers in a way because Paul was already not a stranger."

Sanaa Lathan, who plays the lead character Alexa, was best known for playing Wesley Snipes' mother in Blade. "Well, I read the script and it was a great role," said Lathan. "All of the things that I look for in my jobs were there. All the qualities were there and it was a character that I felt would be challenging to play. She goes through a big change in the movie. It was a very developed storyline and it was something that I had not done before. I had seen a couple of the Alien films but I didn't really remember them. I was really young when I saw them, so it was interesting because it was a last minute thing for me. I had just finished promoting Out of Time and I was on the road and feeling sort of sick. My agent said that I had to go in for this movie and it was on Friday when he told me and the meeting was set for Saturday. I was like, "I don't to want to go in. I'm tired", and he said, "It's a last minute thing. You've got to do it." Literally, within a week, I was in Prague shooting."

The rest of the cast for Alien vs Predator was made up mostly of actors from Europe. Raoul Bova, who plays Professor Sebastian De Rosa, had made a lot of films in Italy. There were no big stars although some reasonably familiar faces like Colin Salmon (who had worked with Anderson on Resident Evil) from the Bond films and Ewan Bremner from Trainspotting. "What I'm really pleased about is the fact that Paul doesn't overuse CGI on it," said Salmon of the film. "We have two actors playing the Alien and the Predator, so we get to face the real thing. The big 'wow' other than seeing the sets, which were amazing, was seeing the Queen alien which arrived from America and was a 30ft robotic machine operated by six Americans on computers. Technology has gone a long way since 25 years ago, so it should be seamless."

Ian Whyte dons the Predator suit in the film and would return for the sequel. The 7'1 Whyte would also play an 'Engineer' in Ridley Scott's Prometheus. Arnold Schwarzenegger was apparently going to have a cameo as 'Dutch' in Alien vs Predator but had to bail out when he was elected the governor of California. Anderson made the film in Prague and had a $50 million budget. The reason why the film was made in Prague was money. Anderson said it would have cost them a lot more to build the same sets in Hollywood. Austrian composer Harald Kloser was chosen to do the music.

Marc Cerasini, who wrote the novelisation for the film, said the there were many script problems - which made his task all the more challenging. "When I was asked to do the novelisation I was sent an early draft and told it was an early draft. It had the Cambodia opening, and there was some confusion about whether the present-day action took place on the North or South Pole. There were five Predators, and Sebastian was not Italian. The second script I received was supposedly the shooting script. There were still five Predators, the Cambodia stuff was gone, replaced by the whaling prologue which I was told not to write because it was filmed but would be cut.

"Alexa the heroine had a prior relationship with Quinn, one of the mercenaries hired by Charles Weyland. Sebastian was now Italian, but the character Miller was from Cleveland, Ohio, not Scotland, and that is how I wrote him. There is an epilogue where someone gets hold of a Predator weapon and it is turned over to executives at Weyland-Yutani Corporationn. There was still confusion about whether we were at the North or South Pole, but I wrote the tie in figuring it was the South Pole, and made the tracked vehicles orange (as they are in Antarctica, by international law). Both polar bears and penguins were mentioned in the script so I wrote them in. Of course polar bears and penguins don't live on the same pole, but I wrote as scripted with the intention of cutting later (see below why those cuts never happened).

"There were other changes — the ice tunnel was shaped differently from the script to the movie. People died in a different order, etc. In the script I wrote from there is a huge underground battle between the surviving four Predators, the humans, and the horde of Aliens that escape the pyramid. In a prior sequence the Predator who is slain gives birth to an Alien hybrid and that creature joins the fray (which is in my novel) – all of this is not in the final cut of the movie, and likely were never filmed. The ending of this version takes place in the old whaling station, with Alexa and the Scar sending the Alien Queen back down the ice hole to the buried city by dumping construction vehicles on top of her. Then the city is blown up, the tunnel sealed forever. I had perhaps a month or six weeks to write an 80-thousand word draft and I finished it on time and turned it in on a Friday.

"That Saturday I got a call from my brother that my father had died suddenly. On Monday as I was packing for the trip home for the funeral, I got a call from my editor that changed everything. Someone at the production company had failed to send me the FINAL draft of the script, which was significantly different from the one I wrote from. I was told that Fox would not approve my tie-in without changes and I had a week to make them. I went to my Dad's funeral, got back on a plane to New York the next day, and rewrote the final draft of AvP in five days. This final script jettisoned the prior relationship between Quinn and Alexa, aka Lex now. Two of the five Predators, and the whole blowing up of the underground city with the Alien Queen inside ending was also gone. Even this final script had Miller as an American, and other small things that ended up changing, probably on set as they filmed."

The omens were never very good for this film if truth be told. It felt like a cheap cash grab and the choice of director was not exactly inspiring. Would Alien vs Predator somehow confound our low expectations though? Well, let's find out.

REVIEW

What is the premise of Alien vs Predator? A billionaire named Charles Weyland (Lance Henricksen), of Weyland Industries, is putting together a team of scientists and mercenaries to investigate a subantarctic heat source emanating from kilometres below the ice. There is a pyramid beneath the surface and Weyland wants to get there first to claim it. It turns out this icy temple is used by Predators to breed alien xenomorphs to hunt. They've been visiting Earth for centuries for this ritual. Weyland and his team are about to end up right in the middle of the carnage...

Alien vs Predator was the first Predator film not to have an R rating and one misses the darkness and gore we associate with this franchise (not that everyone would regard Alien vs Predator to be a true part of the Predator franchise). There are a number of problems with Alien vs Predator but the worst is that it seems like a small film. It isn't set in space or on an alien world. Oh no. It takes place underground on Earth. It feels rather similar to Anderson's first Resident Evil film, another forgettable horror actioner that takes place underground.

Anderson must have liked those Cube films because he's obsessed with characters being trapped in maze like structures. So you get all these constrictive studio bound backdrops of characters lost in these underground traps and in the end it just becomes tedious. A lot of the time you can barely make out what is supposed to be happening. The special effects are hardly awe inspiring and make the film look cheap.

There is always a vaguely rushed feeling to Alien vs Predator that makes you feel as if you are watching a film that was never quite finished. It had an incredibly tight production schedule by all accounts with eight weeks allocated to shooting and a short post-production. Everything feels somewhat undercooked. The special effects and monster designs could be better and the screenplay feels like it needs another draft or two. The characters need to be more fleshed out and the casting in this film, for the most part, could be considered something of a disaster.

One of the most important things about films like this is that they need memorable characters in order to succeed. It's why Alien and Aliens are held in such high regard. It's why the original Predator is held in such high regard. Those films had great characters and they were superbly cast films too. Alien vs Predator has absolutely no memorable characters whatsoever. Sanaa Lathan doesn't have much charisma as the heroine Alexa Woods (who is vaguely patterned after Machiko Noguchi from the comics and is given the mark of the Predator) and gives a rather wooden performance. Her heart doesn't really seem to be the film. Alexa is a dull heroine in this movie.

A lot of the actors in this film sound like they are reading their lines off cue cards. You suspect (whether fairly or unfairly) that many of them are not invested at all and are well aware that this film isn't very good. Colin Salmon plays the same character he plays in nearly everything (as the suave soldier Max Stafford) while Ewen Bremner, like Lathan, seems vaguely embarrassed to be in the film. Bremner plays the main scientist in the team - Dr Miller. Some of Bremner's line readings are so awful it is beyond belief.

The European actors who pad out the cast are terribly wooden. No one in the cast has any chemistry at all. There is no charisma on show save for Lance Henricksen. Lance Henricksen is always great but once he departs from the story there are no charismatic actors left to play this very weak material. The film ends up with Lathan teaming up with a Predator to battle the xenomorphs and escape. It's a logical if obvious idea to make the Predators unlikely allies given that they have technology and a code of honour (of sorts) - as opposed to the unfathomable xenomorphs.

The comics had an obvious advantage in that they were only limited by the writer's imagination and the artist could depict anything. This film version seems as if its main priority was to keep the costs down. A film like this, in order to work, probably had to be strange and futuristic and have much more of an edge. It needed to be less Resident Evil and more Starship Troopers. It needed to take us into space and onto alien worlds. Far flung humans in the future stumbling across these two fearsome species. Anderson's film is very studio bound and formulaic. It doesn't give us much visual spectacle or bring anything new to the table as far as the Alien and Predator franchises go.

Another much cited problem is that the film is somewhat murky looking and this (and the editing) makes it so you can hardly tell what is happening at times. The xenomorph v Predator fights take an age to arrive and never really hit the mark. When a Predator starts swinging an alien around by its feet like it's a WWE wrestling match you know that the film is never going to work and has more or less given up. It's fun at first to see these two legendary monsters encounter one another but the novelty quickly wears off as they battle in the cramped underground pyramid sets in the gloom.

The xenomorph/Predator fights soon become quite repetitive. So, basically, this grand high concept that was supposed to be such a surefire thing actually turns out to be surprisingly boring in reality. Maybe this could concept could have worked with a better director and more money behind it but it definitely doesn't work in this movie.

The best sequence in the film comes when the Predators stealthily take out some of Weyland's men above ground at the whaling station. The Predators are much more frightening when they use cunning and their invisible technology. This is one of the few sequences in the film that is worthy of a bona fide Predator movie as it makes the Predators lethal and scary - just as they should be.

Sadly though the Predators are rather diluted in the end by having to share a film with the xenomorphs (not to mention a large collection of forgettable human characters). You get facehuggers and an Alien Queen thrown into the story but the film never really brings anything new to the universes involving these creatures or ever really justifies its existence. It feels like a film going through the motions. Alien vs Predator feels like a fanmade computer game which uses assets from more famous and vastly superior games. It does neither the Predators nor the xenomorphs justice.

Alien vs Predator riffs on Alien and Aliens (the briefing scene is a direct copy from Aliens) but it never feels as if it has earned the references and use of these iconic monsters. They feel thrown in for the sake of it in a forgettable action film that never feels ambitious. With respect to Paul W. S. Anderson, his presence as the director in the first place does tend to cloud our expectations and give substance to the suspicion that this was always going to be a quick moneymaking exercise rather than something that was willing to take any risks. Anderson is a very B-list director and Alien vs Predator feels very by the numbers and more or less exactly what we might expect from him.

The main Predator they use here feels far too lumbering. Predators need to be lighter on their feet and used more sparingly. The more you see of the Predator in the film the more you become aware that it's just a big actor in a suit. Keep the Predators in the shadows more. Alien vs Predator is unlikely to satisfy either action or horror fans and is not a film that stays in the memory very long. They were probably on a hiding to nothing even attempting to make this film in the first place but the execution leaves a lot to be desired and all but assured a hostile reception from both film critics and fans of the comic.

Alien vs Predator was always a compromised project that had scant chance of producing a great movie. It had a modest budget and a stipulation from Fox that it had to be set on present day Earth to keep the costs down (this is why Anderson set the film underground in Antarctica - it was the most alien environment he could think of on Earth). Worst of all though was the stipulation from the studio that Alien vs Predator had to be a PG-13 in order to have access to the widest possible audience.

Although this made sense from a strictly commercial point of view (the studio probably also had an eye on attracting young gamers who had enjoyed the Alien vs Predator video games) it meant the film came across as tame and bland to anyone who had grown up watching the first two Predator movies and Alien and Aliens. The horror and gore we associate with these franchises was gone. These two iconic movie monsters feel diluted and wasted in the film.

There was an unrated cut of Alien vs Predator but it barely added much at all and didn't improve the film to any noticeable degree. Another big problem with Alien vs Predator was the chintzy CGI. The days of old school practical effects (which had made the early Alien and Predator films so memorable) were well and truly gone by now. Alien vs Predator was not screened for critics (this is obviously a standard firefighting tactic by studios who know they have a mediocre film on their hands) and got fairly terrible reviews when everyone finally got a chance to see it. It ended up with just 22% on Rotten Tomatoes.

Here's the thing though. The Alien vs Predator brand (or curiosity if you will) and lower certificate actually worked as a commercial strategy. The film grossed $177 million - which made it much more profitable than the last stand alone Alien and Predator movies. This meant that we were going to get a sequel. The real Predator franchise, dormant since 1990, was left to gather more dust and cobwebs while Fox attempted to wring the last remaining pennies out of the AvP concept.

We should point out at this juncture that not everyone hated Alien vs Predator. Some people thought it was harmless fun and perfectly entertaining for what it was. No one would pretend it was a great film though like the first two Alien films and the first Predator film had been. Alien vs Predator, at best, was more in line with Anderson's Resident Evil films. Mildly diverting at times but instantly forgettable.

It is obviously difficult to fit the two Alien v Predator films into the Predator franchise or even the Alien franchise) because they represent an interlude - a diversion if you will. These two films were made at a point where Fox didn't really know what to do with the Predator or Alien franchises and were not sure if there was a market for either. So they decided to finally give the AvP concept a whirl. It's best to just think of these two AvP films as their own thing.

Alien vs Predator is not the worst film ever made. It is watchable if you stumble across it late at night and don't have anything better to do. It is though a far cry from the early Alien and Predator films and even Alien 3. I'm not the biggest fan of Alien 3 but that film is clearly bold and well made. It takes risks and has plenty of talent on both sides of the camera. The worst thing about Alien vs Predator is the lack of ambition. You can see they just wanted a film that would be quick to make and wouldn't cost too much money. The film made a profit but the bad reviews and the monster mash-up concept tarnished both the Alien and Predator brands. It would get even worse with the next film.

* Many years later, Briggs said - "My version of Alien vs Predator, a spec screenplay I wrote in the Summer of 1991, was the very first draft, the very first piece of actual work done on the project for the studio. It was also my first professional sale to 20th Century Fox through producers Lawrence Gordon and Lloyd Levin, with whom I'd go on to work on Judge Dredd (another tortuous Development Hell story) and as credited co-writer on the Hellboy movie in 2004.

"It's fair to say that despite my draft remaining unfilmed, Alien vs Predator launched my career; high-profile enough to get me mentioned in a slew of magazines and books like Chris Gore's The 50 Greatest Movies Never Made, and Denny Martin Flynn's How Not To Write A Screenplay (alongside my friend Shane Black's Lethal Weapon.) A decade-and-change later in 2004, I discovered to my astonishment in going over the project's materials at the Writers' Guild arbitration for the Paul WS Anderson movie at the WGA headquarters on Fairfax, my work was also the only actual complete screenplay Fox had until Paul WS Anderson initiated his attempt over a decade later!

"To follow the chronology, the Dark Horse Alien vs Predator comic title itself, which gave me that initial kick in the backside to write a story mostly different from its inspirational material, ran July to December 1990. Principal photography on the Alien 3 movie began one month later in January 1991. Although the (excellent) Rex Pickett rewrite for director David Fincher from this time had Ripley dying, I gather this was also something the prior director Vincent Ward, whom Fincher replaced, had also wanted in his drafts. I lived in London at the time, and wangled an Alien 3 set visit at the shoot's end as guest of Amalgamated Dynamics FX shop owners Alec Gillis and Tom Woodruff. With film journalist friend Juhani Nurmi, we'd concocted a crazy notion to introduce Alien designer genius HR Giger to Finnish director Renny Harlin, who was the attached Alien 3 director prior to Vincent Ward. Juhani was a longtime friend of both, and made the introduction. Giger would carry on (quite vocally in interviews) through the finished film.

"After being shown the Pinewood Creature Shop (production all-but over at this point), Alec, Tom and myself sat around yakking fanboy stuff and discussing the difficult shoot. They said they hadn't seen Predator 2 at that juncture, but had heard about Danny Glover seeing the Alien skull cameo in the Predator trophy room scene at the movie's end. Alec knew I was a struggling writer (developing sci-fi material for the short-lived Paramount UK at the time) and asked what I was working on. Tom arched an eyebrow (neither were aware of the Dark Horse comic) when I said I'd just started writing Alien vs Predator as a spec script. "Man, I can't see how that would happen!" remarked Alec; amusing in retrospect given Amalgamated Dynamics ended up doing outstanding work on both of the Alien vs Predator spinoffs.

"I finished my Alien vs Predator draft late September 1991. It was literally only written as a "get attention" sample, in the hope I'd maybe get a rewrite on some other movie off the back of it. My then-agent (Steve Kenis, the head of the William Morris agency in London) was friendly with producer Larry Gordon, who had a deal with Fox. Steve was coincidentally flying over to the States for meetings. Steve met Larry. They talked. I remember sitting heavily down on the stairs when Steve phoned me from L.A. to tell me Larry bought the script the same day. And then round-after-tortured-round of additional producer in-fighting killed the project dead on that go-around during the next year. (I was told later there was even serious talk about tweaking the project to make it a Schwarzenegger vehicle: Arnie was briefly attached to the pre-Stallone version of Judge Dredd I worked on for Tony Scott, so I can only imagine how that would have gone. More recently, the Strause Brothers in interview at the time of their Requiem sequel admitted they'd toyed with attempting my more-expensive outer-space, more sci-fi script, but went instead for the different Earthbound story you saw on the screen in 2007.)

"Larry Gordon would later tell me Alien vs Predator had only been discussed for the first time at Fox literally days before Steve gave him the script in September 1991, which is why I was in the right place at the right time to make my first sale. Maybe they were in a panic about Alien 3...I have no idea. And so when I hear Sigourney Weaver recounting her killing off Ripley in Alien 3 because she'd heard Fox were talking about doing Alien vs Predator, despite the fact our project was first spoken about and initiated well over a year (not even counting Vincent Ward's involvement!) after her movie had gone into active production, I really have to roll my eyes at her claims.

"I love Alien 3. Well; I didn't on its theatrical release, but I find the recent extended DVD recut even more watchable than Aliens. I'll also be honest that I'm less-than-wild about the two Alien vs Predator movies (particularly Requiem, about which less said the better) But I do wish Sigourney Weaver would stop beating on Alien vs Predator as her pet piñata in "ruining" the Alien franchise, and acknowledge that two standalone Alien movies she was actively involved with unfortunately managed that first, all on their own. I don't even know if Sigourney Weaver has read the Alien vs Predator draft I wrote. She's never said she has. But, I was a fan obsessive of the Alien franchise, Sigourney. Big time. Particularly Ridley's original, which is still unmatched. And Alien vs Predator — as a concept — is still killer, full of potential. Even its critically maligned first cinematic outing made $172,544,654 worldwide, compared to $159,814,498 for Alien 3 and $161,376,068 for "Resurrection". Hardly a financial "fail" there, Sigourney. There's a terrific Alien vs Predator movie still to be made by someone. It just hasn't happened yet."

** Event Horizon is 1997 sci-fi horror film. You could make a solid case for this being the best film that Anderson has directed. The film is about an expedition to find a missing ship called 'Event Horizon' which has suddenly re-appeared near Neptune. It transpires that the Event Horizon had experimental engine technology and when it was activated it may have warped into another dimension. The crew of the ship mutilated each other and all went insane. Could it be that the Event Horizon opened a portal to Hell? Event Horizon started life as much more of an Alien homage but the final script pivoted it towards Hellraiser too so some of the pure Alien DNA was lost. It's still clearly a film that loves the Alien franchise though and the gothic elements vaguely evoke Alien 3. What links Event Horizon and Alien is the intent to make a haunted house film in space. There's a great cast here too with Laurence Fishburne, Sam Neil, Jason Isaacs, Kathleen Quinlan, and Joely Richardson. Event horizon is a decent horror space thriller and one of the few Paul W. S Anderson films that you might actually encourage people to watch.

ALIENS VS PREDATOR: REQUIEM (2007)

Despite the decidedly tepid critical reception of the first Alien vs Predator film, the box-office takings meant we got a sequel - this time directed by The Brothers Strause. The Brothers Strause are Greg and Colin Strause. They started as special effects experts and worked on a raft of big films including The X-Files. The duo also directed a number of music videos. They later directed a dreadful science fiction film called Skyline after doing the Alien vs

Predator sequel. If they'd directed Skyline before the AvP sequel came up you'd have to presume they wouldn't have got the gig in the first place.

Given their background and expertise in special effects, the Strause brothers were seen by Fox as people who would be able to keep costs to a minimum but also deliver a professional looking film. "Yeah, it happened pretty quickly," said Colin Strause. "We met all of the executives over at Fox. And we'd been doing a lot of work for them. Just a ton of stuff over the years. We pitched on Wolfenstein. Then when this came around, it was all the exact same people. We got our hands on it. We had about a week to put together a visual presentation. We had one really good meeting. And then two other meetings after that."

An early plan by the film's writer Shane Salerno had the Predator taking on a special forces team in Afghanistan (how the xenomorphs would have been shoehorned into this premise is anyone's guess) but Fox vetoed this idea as they felt it might be too expensive for the budget they had in mind. The Strauses were given a budget of forty million dollars (considerably less than that allocated to Paul W. S Anderson on the previous film). Despite their grandiose early plans ("Our first pitch was like Dances with Wolves. There was going to be forty-five minutes where there were no spoken lines in the movie. We tried...") the duo were told by Fox that the film had to take place on Earth in a small town in the present day so that it wouldn't be too expensive.

It was deja vu. Fox were basically making these AvP films on the cheap. The law of diminishing returns. One has the impression that Fox didn't think the Alien vs Predator films were going to have an especially long shelf life so mitigated this by slashing the budget on the second one. The general law with sequels in Hollywood is that you throw more money at them and make them bigger films than the original. Fox were doing the complete opposite! The thought of an Alien vs Predator sequel AGAIN set on Earth in the present day wasn't exactly the most exciting news.

"Well, I mean, the thing we were trying to be careful of is we didn't want to have Aliens dancing in front of McDonald's and stuff. I know a lot of people were worried being on Earth it's like you know what are the locations going to be," said Colin Strause. "One of the first things in our pitch we said the movie's got to take place and power's going get knocked out and it's got to be raining the whole last night. Seeing an Alien in broad daylight or just plain view is going to look stupid no matter what you do. The reason it worked in all the other movies is you were in a dark spaceship, you had flashing blinking lights, steam jets. You had all these great elements to cover them up basically and if you don't do that they're going to look like guys in suits.

"That's why the first thing we did is get that atmosphere and that in there and the 2nd thing was picking cooler locations. The 1st big battle takes place in this huge underground sewer network. The next battle takes place in a power plant. Then you have the big rooftop battle. Then there's a National Guard battle on the street in the rain. We tried to pick locations that even though they were earth bound, they still were reminiscent of you know, the power plant is going to look very much like Alien. It's got all the yellow warning beacons and lot of steam and everything so we're trying to give it that space sort of feel so even though it is Earth it doesn't—try not to make it feel cheesy or anything, just give it a much more gritty kind of environments."

Liam O'Donnell, who worked closely with the Strauses, later seemed to imply that no one on the production was too thrilled about having to make a film set in present day Earth in a small town but they didn't have any choice. In contrast to the first Alien vs Predator film, the Strauses promised that their Alien vs Predator movie would be R-rated and have the gore and scares of the old Alien and Predator films. "We tried to make a good scary film," said Colin. "We tried to treat it not as a versus movie. People think that those are kind of cheesy. We tried to keep it as real as we could with some of the creatures. We wanted to make a good, scary, dark movie. Our goal was to make The Texas Chainsaw Massacre with scary creatures. That is the tone of it."

"We felt that if anything, over time, maybe the Alien movies had become less and less scary," added Greg Strause. "And we thought it was very important to bring back all of the elements that made the first Alien and Aliens the scary, visceral experiences they were. We wanted the whole second half of the movie to be at night. We wanted it to be raining. We're trying to add atmosphere. [The movie is set] in a small town. We don't have all the tools at our disposal that Ridley [Scott] had inside the spaceship [of Alien]. He was just a master – using steam and flashing lights and whatnot to create that incredible, horrific tension. So, we tried to figure out as many was as we could in an exterior small town setting to do that. Halfway through the movie, the power goes out. There's no lights anywhere. We used all these classic horror techniques, we tried to inject into this film. There's actual jump scares– Aliens that are actually gonna scare the hell out of people again."

Shane Salerno's script for Aliens vs Predator: Requiem must have leaked because it was reviewed on Ain't It Cool in 2006. Ain't It Cool appears to be defunct these days but back in 2006 it was the place to go to for film scoops and nerdy debate about movies. Reviewing the script for AIC, 'Moriarty' wrote - 'It's catastrophic. It's really that bad a script. If fans don't already feel like whipped dogs, they will by the end of this, and the sad thing is, they'll buy just enough tickets to guarantee Fox makes another one of these, if only for DVD, in the future. Because it's so cold and crass and calculating, so pointless a retread of the work of the genuine talents involved in the franchises previously, this is the one that feels like the stake in the heart of both properties. This is the announcement that they're not remotely interested in continuing the films in a way that expands the great work that already exists. It's creatively bankrupt in a way designed to take the least effort for a return. It's a bitter pill to swallow, having to kiss off both franchises for the time being, and all I can hope is that there's a genuine rebirth later. This certainly isn't it.'

Production of Aliens vs Predator: Requiem began in Vancouver in 2006. The film had a 52 day shooting schedule and snow was a pesky nuisance at times. The cast assembled for the film contained no famous or instantly recognisable names. The budget simply didn't allow for hiring any big stars and it is highly doubtful that any big stars would have wanted to be in this film anyway even if they been paid a handsome salary. If the first film had a B list cast you could say that Requiem had a D list cast.

Reiko Aylesworth, the Ripley-esque looking female lead, was best known for her role on the television series 24 as Michelle Dessler. The male lead Steven Pasquale was best known for his role in the FX show Rescue Me about firefighters. John Ortiz, who plays Sheriff Eddie Morales, was a film and television veteran and later appeared in a couple of the Fast & Furious movies. Johnny Lewis, who plays Ricky Howard, would later become best known for the television show Sons of Anarchy. Sadly, Johnny Lewis died in strange circumstances in 2012 aged just 28. Sam Trammell, who plays Tim O'Brien, would later became best known for his role in the television show True Blood.

Bill Paxton, Danny Glover and Adam Baldwin from Predator 2 were sought to appear in Aliens vs Predator: Requiem but nothing came of this. Michael Biehn was apparently going to play a soldier at the end of the film but Fox blocked this knowing piece of stunt casting. The Predalien hybrid in the film was nicknamed "Chet" on set and in the script. This was to avoid early spoilers about the nature of the creature. Chet is a reference from the John Hughes film Weird Science.

The Predator was known as Wolf to the crew because - like Harvey Keitel in Pulp Fiction - he's on a mission to mask evidence and clean up a mess. The Strauses did nearly all of the special effects shots with their own in-house company and certainly talked a good game when promotion for the film began. They promised fans a rip-roaring blood soaked good time at the cinema. Would the actual film live up to their promises? Let's find it.

In the plot of Aliens vs Predator: Requiem, a chestburster that is a hybrid Alien/Predator erupts from Scar (the Predator from the first film) on a Predator ship. It grows into a 'Predalien' and in the commotion the scout ship it is on crashes in a forest near Gunnison, Colorado. A lone Predator picks up the distress signal and sets off for Earth to kill the Predalien and clean up the mess and inevitable xenomorph infestation. Needless to say, a plucky band of local inhabitants are going to become embroiled in the danger and mayhem...

What can we possibly say about Aliens vs Predator: Requiem? Aliens v Predator: Requiem put this fledgling new franchise to bed and buried it in concrete. As Peter Briggs said, a great Alien vs Predator film was possible. There was always potential. Sadly, Aliens vs Predator: Requiem is about as far away from a great Alien vs Predator film as it is possible to get. The film repeats the tactic of the first Alien v Predator by having the action set on Earth. Why were these films never set in outer space or on an alien world? Money, as we have already mentioned, is the obvious answer. So instead of a futuristic Alien v Predator smackdown in the far flung corners of space the story takes place in a small town on Earth. There are large chunks of the film where you wouldn't even know this was supposed to be an Alien vs Predator movie if you wandered in at a random time!

What the two Alien vs Predator films do seem to confirm is that you can't make a success of this concept on the cheap. If you truly want to make a great Alien vs Predator film you've got to be prepared to spend more money and - with all respect - hire more talented and inventive directors than Paul W. S Anderson or the Brothers Strause. In a sense these films were already doomed before they arrived. No one expected them to be any good. There was no great buzz or anticipation. No one thought that Paul W. S Anderson or The Strause Brothers were capable of making a film to stand alongside the best entries in the Alien and Predator franchises - especially with the less than stratospheric budgets allocated to them. These assumptions all turned to be true. It was inevitable.

The basic premise in Requiem of a xenomorph infestation abounding in the small town and a Predator being dispatched to go and clean up the mess doesn't bring anything new to this short lived franchise. We already saw Predators fighting the xenomorphs in the first film so that particular novelty is gone. The brief shot of the Predator at home being alerted to the xenomorph outbreak and grabbing one of those Predator helmets as he leaves is fun at least. This is the only time in any franchise we ever got a glimpse of a Predator at home.

What do Predators do when they aren't slaughtering and hunting on alien worlds? Do they have a Predator version of television with gameshows and sitcoms? Do they have Predator garden parties where they all eat cakes and make small talk? Joking aside, it would be fascinating to get a glimpse of what the Predator society is like - although probably unwise because you don't want to demystify the Predators too much. In one of the Predator comics the Predator homeworld is depicted as a barren rocky place where the Predators live in little tribes like Native Americans. In this movie though the Predator homeworld is depicted as some technological utopia.

It's fun to see a Predator in a more relaxed environment and it does make you wonder what a film set in or around the Predator world might have been like. A lot more interesting than Aliens vs Predator: Requiem one would imagine. Do all Predators venture into the stars to hunt other species or is it just a select group? Are there Predators who disapprove of this hunting custom - just as there are many humans who find the idea of killing animals for meat or hunting them for sport distasteful, barbaric, cruel and unnecessary? Who knows but it might be interesting to explore - even at the risk of losing some of the Predator mystique.

Because the Predators have highly advanced technology and space travel they are clearly a vastly intelligent species who must have scientists, engineers, and advanced medicine. Their home planet must be a technological marvel that humans can barely comprehend. Aliens vs Predator: Requiem features a forgettable collection of small town teens who run foul of the alien outbreak and then seems to focus a lot on the Predator as he tries to stop the outbreak without being discovered. It's modestly diverting at first to watch the Predator in action but it becomes awfully repetitive very fast and the lighting in some of these scenes is ridiculous.

The first film was murky and this is even worse. Aliens vs Predator: Requiem is so badly lit you can't actually see what is supposed to be happening on the screen half the time! Even the people who made this film later complained about the colour grading themselves! They said the film was not supposed to be this dark and it had nothing to with them.

The Predator in Aliens vs Predator: Requiem seems to spend far too much time in a sewer. Not only do these dimly lit locations make the film feel constrictive, they also smother the action and make everything seem small scale. It probably wouldn't have cost that much money to build a few spaceship corridors sets and set the film in outer space.

One thinks of how inventive the bargain budget Roger Corman space thrillers like Forbidden World and Galaxy of Terror were with absolutely no money whatsoever at their disposal. Aliens vs Predator: Requiem might have been fun as a spaceship set B-movie. No classic for sure but much more of a guilty pleasure than we get here. Because these Alien vs Predator films are never set in alien worlds or in outer space they had to therefore find weird and claustrophobic environments on Earth. Paul W. S Anderson set his film underground. Requiem tries to get around the bland present day Earth locations by having all these scenes in sewer tunnels!

The younger characters in the film seem inserted by a formula bound studio directive. Someone, somewhere, has stipulated that the film must feature young characters for the young audiences they want to entice. They've stipulated that the film must reside in an everday American town on Earth so that (1) it won't be an expensive film to make and (2) will be a more relatable experience. Or something along these lines. Alien vs Predator had very forgettable characters but it did at least have Lance Henricksen and a few familiar faces. Aliens vs Predator: Requiem has absolutely nothing on this front. It's hard to even remember what anyone is called in this film. You honestly could not care less about a single character in Alien vs Predator: Requiem!

The biggest difference between this and the first Alien vs Predator film is that the nastiness factor is increased considerably. They seem to go out of their way in this one to shock at times. The start of the film has a father and son in the woods stumbling across some facehuggers and both ending up with a facehugger impaled on their face. Heartless! Later on, in a disgusting scene, a pregnant woman in hospital is forcibly mouth raped by the Predator/Alien hybrid creature. This is a really mean spirited film - and not in a good satiric Paul Verhoven sort of way. The balance is completely wrong. Who thought it was a good idea to have an intense and grotesque horror sequence in a maternity ward?

You can pinpoint where the film and the directors have completely given up because they start making Ripley lookalike Reiko Aylesworth pose with a Newtesque child and start using riffs from James Horner's Aliens score. There's even a rip-off of the APC from Aliens. It's such a self defeating direction to go in. Why remind us of Aliens? All you are doing is reminding us of how much better that film is! It's completely pointless. Even action sequences that sound fun on paper - like the xenomorphs attacking the National Guard - are staged and directed in a flat and unimaginative way. You can barely see anything during this sequence and rather than be its own thing the sequence is desperate to mimic the sequence in Aliens where the Colonial Marines first encounter the aliens and nearly get wiped out.

Take, by way of contrast, the sequence in Predator 2 where Keyes and his men try to capture the Predator in the meat warehouse. This sequence is also inspired by the Marines v xenomorphs sequence in Aliens (we know that for a fact because Stephen Hopkins said as much) but it doesn't try to be a carbon copy and so stands as a good sequence in its own right. Aliens vs Predator: Requiem is desperate to remind us of Aliens but this approach seems completely pointless because Aliens was lightning in a bottle. Why try to mimic a good film in a bad film?

Is there anything at all positive to say about Aliens vs Predator: Requiem? Well, the central Predator known as 'Wolf' does have some personality and is fairly well done. It's hard to have a sympathetic Predator but we sort of root for Wolf because he's basically just trying to clean up a giant mess. It's just a shame though that this particular Predator is in such a terrible film. Setting the film in an ordinary small town though just doesn't work. It makes the film look and seem generic - despite all the Predator and xenomorph carnage thrown at the screen. What is incredible is that a decade later Shane Black would make exactly the same mistake with The Predator.

Aliens vs Predator: Requiem has no sense of pacing, no character building, little to no story, and plays more like an elaborate fan film than a mainstream Hollywood release. Aliens vs Predator: Requiem gropes its way to a predictable conclusion (that completely rips off Return of the Living Dead) and by the end it has done something truly remarkable. It has made Paul W. S Anderson almost look good in retrospect. Aliens vs Predator: Requiem is probably worth at least one late night watch for the very curious but ultimately this is a very mediocre and forgettable film that has a slipshod aura and a story that feels like they were just making it up as they went along.

There are too many characters in Requiem, the characters are boring, the acting is telephoned in, and the Predator fighting xenomorphs already got old fast in the last film. Alarm bells soon began to chime when Aliens vs Predator: Requiem, like its predecessor, was not screened for critics. This is a standard ruse by studios when they know they have a clunker on their hands and want to avoid a rush of advance negative reviews. The film was predictably savaged by critics - only mustering a meagre 12% on Rotten Tomatoes. Aliens vs Predator: Requiem is a terrible film that made sure this particular high concept would not return in the foreseeable future. Even those with low expectations and a sweet tooth for low-budget sci-fi horror could find little in Aliens vs Predator: Requiem to satiate their curiosity.

Despite the abysmal reviews, Aliens vs Predator: Requiem made around $130 million at the box-office so it was far from a financial bust. The studio must have at least considered the possibility of cranking out a third AvP film. Liam O'Donnell actually wrote a treatment for a proposed third Alien vs Predator film. The treatment was set in the future on an Earth ravaged by climate change and has Weyland-Yutani dominant - having created something akin to a one world government. The only haven of freedom left is a part of Africa - where people flock to try and escape from the oppressive totalitarian conditions of other nations. This part of Africa though has a precious mineral that Weyland-Yutani need. Into the midst of all of this tension is thrown a Predator - now on safari in Africa.

The Brothers Strause also pitched an idea for Alien vs Predator 3. "The original ending for AVP: Requiem, that we pitched them, ended up on the alien homeward, and actually going from the Predator gun, that you see at the end, it was going to transition from that gun to a logo of a Weyland-Yutani spaceship that was heading to an alien planet," Greg Strause told Gizmodo. "And then we were actually going to cut down to the surface [of the alien planet] and you were going to see a hunt going on. It was going to be a whole tribe of predators going against this creature that we called 'King Alien.'

"It's this huge giant winged alien thing. And that was going to be the lead-in, to show that the fact that the Predator gun [at the end of AVP: Requiem] is the impetus of all the technological

advancements that allowed humans to travel in space. Which leads up to the Alien timeline. That was the whole idea, was to literally continue from Ms. Yutani getting the gun – and then cut to 50 years in the future, and there's spaceships now," Strause added. We've made a quantum leap in space travel. That was going to set up the ending, which would then set up what AVP was going to be, which would take place 100 years in the future. That was kind of the plan."
for now

Thankfully though, common sense prevailed and Fox did not attempt to squeeze out a third AvP film. Two was quite enough for now thank you very much. Maybe one day someone will make a great Alien vs Predator film but it was time to put this hybrid franchise into storage for a good while. The end of this strange detour in the story of the Alien and Predator franchises was welcome because it meant the studio finally started thinking about making a new Predator film. We hadn't seen a Predator film since 1990 so it was high time for this iconic creature to get a solo spotlight again.

PREDATORS (2010)

As we discussed earlier, Predator 2 was not a success and drew mostly negative reviews and a very modest box office take. The departure of Arnold Schwarzenegger had effectively killed both the film and the franchise it seemed. However, in 1994, long before the AvP films, 20th Century Fox asked Robert Rodriguez to write a new Predator screenplay for them while he was waiting to shoot Desperado. The story (which began on a Spanish galleon ship) he gave the studio was deemed too expensive to go into production (especially after the weak returns of the second film) and so the property was mothballed. It seems that the studio didn't really know what to do with the Predator franchise at this time.

The script by Rodriguez had Arnie's character Dutch arrested by the military for desertion and taken to Arkus 6 - which turns out to be a sort of Predator big game reserve. There are numerous Predators and other sorts of aliens too on Arkus 6. Somewhat confusingly, despite featuring Dutch, the script is an outer space futuristic sort of romp. It reads a lot like a script that Rodriguez never expected to be made. Not only would it be incredibly expensive to make with all the space scenes and different aliens, the script is also rather preposterous. The script reads a lot like fan fiction but the central premise of a Predator big game reserve is a great concept and would remain intact when a third Predator film finally went into production many years later.

There was another script (by Sam Park) which had Dutch returning and being hunted by Predators during a blizzard in New York. Alex Litvak, who eventually co-wrote 2010's Predators, pitched an idea in the late 1990s where Dutch would lead a team to a mountain range where a Predator ship has crashed. The team would be wiped out - leading Dutch to battle the aliens alone. It would turn out that this was all an elaborate Predator trap so they could hunt Dutch. The main problem with the script treatments for Predator 3 was that they all tended to feature Dutch. However, whenever anyone had a meeting with Arnold Schwarzenegger to discuss one of these ideas it usually became apparent in the end that he was either unavailable or not especially interested.

The other problem was that these scripts would very expensive to produce and Predator 2 hadn't done good numbers at the box-office. As a consequence of this the studio were wary of plunging into Predator 3 - especially without Arnold. By the late 1990s though Arnold was no longer as big a star as he used to be. Films like Eraser and Junior were not as iconic as his old movies and his turn as Mr Freeze in Batman & Robin was widely panned. Arnold had enjoyed a good ten years as Hollywood's biggest star but 1997 was more or less the end of his run at the top. A few years later he went into politics.

Around the time of Predator 2, Stan Winston's iconic Predators enjoyed a new lease of life in comic books - pitted against HR Giger's even more famous creation in the Alien vs Predator series. When the Alien franchise fizzled out with a whimper in the nineties the studio (sadly and unavoidably) decided to use the comic book premise to merge their two defunct former cash cows and so we got the Alien vs Predator films in 2004 and 2007. It was like an update of Universal ensemble monster films or Godzilla vs King Kong and merely diminished the creatures created by Giger and Winston further. The greatest indignity was that had they had to appear in a Paul W. S Anderson film shot on a cheapjack budget with a PG-13 certificate. The spine ripping salad days seemed to be over.

Perhaps it was guilt (and pursuit of a sort of redemption!) but in 2009 Rodriguez was unexpectedly contacted by the studio and asked if he would like to make a new Predator film loosely based on the old screenplay he had given them over a decade before. Fox didn't like the futuristic spaceship stuff in the script but they did like the 'big game preserve' idea and the concept of different types of Predator who are involved in some sort of internal conflict. The story was refined by Alex Litvak and Michael Finch. One of the main concepts was that the Predators in the film would be involved in some sort of blood feud. The script went through several revisions until it was finished.

Something which constricted the writers was that Predators only had a $40 million budget. To put that in perspective, other franchise movies of this era like new Pirates of the Caribbean and Harry Potter entries had budgets of $250 million and $370 million respectively. Predators was made on a shoestring compared to the mainstream Hollywood blockbusters. Fox wanted a new Predator film but they were not willing to gamble or risk too much when it came to money. Predators would then a sort of 'testing the waters' exercise to see if Predator solo films were viable.

Robert Rodriguez was hired as the producer on the film (Rodriguez didn't want to direct Predators himself because he had too much on his slate at the time with Machete and Spy Kids: All the Time in the World) and was given input into who should direct the picture. Neil Marshall, who impressed with Dog Soldiers (which was heavily inspired by the original Predator) and The Descent but then stumbled with Doomsday was a candidate, as was M. J. Bassett - who directed Deathwatch and Silent Hill: Revelation. Marcus Nispel, who directed remakes of The Texas Chainsaw Massacre and Friday the 13th was also considered as was Darren Lynn Bousman. Bousman was best known for his work on the Saw franchise. None of these names, aside perhaps from Marshall (who was quite hot for a time but then went off the boil), were terribly inspiring.

An interesting name thrown into the hat as regards the director was Bill Duke. Duke played Mac in the first Predator film and was an experienced director. Whether or not he would have been a good fit for a sci-fi actioner though is anyone's guess. Most of Bill's films were dramas or comedies although he done a few crime pics with action sequences. The modest budget for Predators was evident in that those in the frame to direct the film were what you might - with respect - describe as B-list names when it came to Hollywood directors.

Perhaps the most intriguing contender to direct Predators was Vincenzo Natali. Natali is best known for the 1997 thriller film Cube (in which a group of characters find themselves trapped in a giant moving maze made up of cubed shape rooms full of deadly traps) and the sci-fi film Splice. Most of Natali's films have got good reviews so you could probably say he had the best batting average of any of the directors in contention.

"Well Predator," said Natali, "that was right after Splice. And so I think people were interested in anything that had a creature in it, like I was on a list. And Predators, which I guess famously began as a script that Robert Rodrigquez had written many years before and was resurrected at Fox...When I was called into pitch, they basically said "we're not using that." There was nothing. There was no script. There was only the notion that this was going to take place on a Predator planet, or another planet. And there was kind of – I think there was a Dangerous Game aspect to it with humans being hunted by Predators.

"And that was literally all that was being presented to me and I just had to go in, and I met with Robert Rodriquez and some executives – separately – and I just did a whole bunch of drawings. I just did drawings. It was actually a really fun project to pitch on because there was nothing...I could just let my imagination go wild. Like whatever crazy Predator image was conjured into my feeble mind I could immediately draw it and present it to them and I wasn't having to adhere to anything they were doing." Natali's design art of humans and other creatures fighting Predators in gladiatorial contests on a spectacular alien world were fantastic but presumably deemed too expensive to put into live action.

In the end Robert Rodriguez chose Nimród Antal to direct Predators. Rodriguez enjoyed Antal's 'snuff' horror thriller Vacancy and selected him on the basis of that. It turned out to be a fairly shrewd choice. None of Antal's movies have got especially good reviews but he has a good feel for action. Despite his fairly modest CV, Nimród Antal is clearly well regarded in the industry because over a decade later the Duffer Brothers hired him to direct two episodes of Stranger Things 4 and they are notoriously picky about who they let direct on that prestigious and lavish show.

The number one choice to play the lead character Royce in Predators was Vin Diesel. Diesel was too occupied though with the Fast and the Furious and getting a third picture in his own outer space Riddick franchise made. This was always an unrealistic target. Diesel would probably have been far too expensive to hire. He may have unbalanced the film too because if your picture is Vin Diesel vs Predator there isn't much tension because you known Diesel is going to win. He isn't going to sign up to a film in which his character's spine is ripped out by a Predator!

The second choice of the producers was Gerard Butler - then riding high at the time due to the success of the film 300. Butler and his management wanted too much money to do Predators though so this option also proved unrealistic. Jamie Fox, Clive Owen, and Michael Fassbender were all offered the lead in Predators and all turned it down. Milo Ventimiglia, Freddy Rodríguez and Josh Brolin were all considered for the lead too but nothing came of any of this. Predators was having a very tricky time finding anyone to play the lead but they eventually found their leading man almost by accident.

During the casting of Predators, Adrien Brody was approached for the part of Edwin - the doctor who turns out to be a serial killer. Brody read the script and asked if he could play the lead character Royce instead. They were happy to agree to this because they didn't have anyone to play Royce and Brody was a fine actor who had the awards to prove it. Robert Rodriguez said Brody was perfect casting because real life soldiers look lean and plausible (as opposed to muscle bound hulks like Arnold Schwarzenegger). Nonetheless, Brody put on 25 pounds of muscle for his role and was game to do as many stunts as possible.

The director Nimrod Antal didn't want a woman in the film but was persuaded to cast Alice Braga as Isabelle. They toyed with the idea of making Alice Braga's character a shapeshifting alien but this idea was jettisoned. The shoot was no picnic for Braga because she had to carry a heavy sniper rifle around. She did some military training to prepare for this. Braga had fairly recently come off an even bigger movie when she starred in I Am Legend with Will Smith.

Apart from Russian Oleg Taktarov (Taktarov is a former mixed martial artist) as Nikolai, a Russian commando from the Spetsnaz Alpha Group, none of the international characters are played by actors from those countries. Alice Braga (who plays a sniper from the Israel Defense Forces) is Brazilian and Louis Ozawa Changchien (a Japanese Yakuza enforcer in the film) and Mahershalalhashbaz "Mahershala" Ali (a death squad soldier from Sierra Leone. in the film) are both American. Mahershala Ali would go on to be an Oscar winning actor - though not for Predators obviously!

When Danny Trejo heard that one of the characters in the film was described as 'looking like Danny Trejo' he contacted the filmmakers and asked for the part! Trejo plays Cuchillo, a Mexican drug cartel enforcer. The talented Walter Goggins was cast as Stans, a highly dangerous death row inmate, and Topher Grace was cast as the doctor Edwin, who seems meek and out of place but turns out to be a Charles Cullen/Ted Bundy style psychopath. Robert Rodriguez wanted to recast Stans because he thought the character was written too much like Hudson from Aliens. Nimrod Antal persuaded him to keep Scoggins in the film - and the character was adjusted.

Topher Grace was wary of taking the part of Edwin at first but decided to do it after reading the script - which he compared to Aliens. This was a pretty amazing cast compared to the AvP movies. None of these actors were superstars but there was an awful lot of acting talent in the Predators ensemble and they weren't finished yet. Laurence Fishburne was also cast in the film - as Noland, a soldier who has somehow survived on the Predator game reserve but has clearly gone doolally in the process. Antal had worked with Fishburne before on the 2009 action film Armored.

Noland was a late addition because the script was too short and didn't have much dialogue. At one point there was a vague idea that the Noland character would be Dutch Schaefer but thankfully this never transpired. It would be a bit depressing to have Dutch come back - only to have gone mad and then be killed off! That would sort of be like Charlton Heston's somewhat depressing cameo in Beneath the Planet of the Apes.

On the question of whether Arnold Schwarzenegger could have been in the film, Robert Rodriguez said - "Early on, since I had worked with Arnold on the original script back in the day and I had spoken with him about it, that was one of the questions I had myself. The world had changed since the last time I worked on this which was '95. In my script he was the entire film and now he was Governor so I was like "I know we can't get him for the lead and I don't even think we can get him for a cameo." We did entertain the idea of where could we place him but as we started putting the script together it really felt like we were making our own film and we thought lets not even bother with him showing up and doing something in it." Apparently there was a plan for Dutch to appear right at the end of the film and say "come with me if you want to live" to Royce and Isabelle.

Predators was filmed in the last months of 2009. The jungle sequences were shot in Hawaii but 60% of the film was shot in Texas to qualify for a tax break. The interiors (Noland's ship refuge) were shot at a studio belonging to Robert Rodriguez. KNB EFX's Howard Berger and Greg Nicotero built the creature suits and John Debny, who had worked with Rodriguez before, composed the score. There would be a range of different Predators in the film. Derek Mears plays the Classic Predator and Brian Steele plays the Berserker and Falconer Predators. Carey Jones plays the Tracker Predator.

The poisonous plant that Edwin mentions in the film is Archaefructus liaoningensis. Archaefructus liaoningensis is an extinct species of flowering plant that lived during the Early Cretaceous period, around 125 million years ago. The creature that chases Edwin in the film early on is an easter egg because the costume is based on the rejected Predator design for the 1987 film. The slightly unusual looking gun that that Adrien Brody's character Royce has in Predators is a AA-12 fully automatic 12 gauge shotgun. The Spetsnaz soldier Nikolai uses a monstrous mini-gun like Jesse Ventura in Predator.

One slightly irritating thing about the preamnble to Predators was that Robert Rodriguez, the writers, and even a few of the cast, seemed to have a few digs at Predator 2. Rodriguez implied that this film would ignore Predator 2 and be a 'true' sequel to the original. Why still no love or respect for Predator 2? For fans like me who enjoy Predator 2 just fine this did all chafe a bit. By the way, there was a comic book tie-in with this film which is worth reading because it isn't an adaptation but a prequel which sets up the events of Predators.

REVIEW

Time has generally been quite kind to Predators. I can remember being distinctly underwhelmed by this picture when it first came out in 2010 but it has grown on me in subsequent viewings and the film, despite a modest budget, is plainly much superior to 2018's The Predator (which we'll obviously discuss shortly) and vastly superior to the two AvP films.

Taking on the Predator this time in the central role is Adrien Brody as a mercenary named Royce. Brody seems a like a strange piece of casting on the face of it but actually works much better than you expect. He overdoes the Christian Bale Batman gravel voice to a ludicrous degree (not quite sure why he decided to do this but then I suppose he's never really been an action star before) but his character is given a cunning, amoral streak that makes him a formidable foe for the extraterrestrial hunters.

Royce is not averse to using other humans as bait and uses his military experience to give himself an understanding of what tactics the Predators might employ and why they do certain things. Royce seems to have more of an intellect and less of a moral compass than Dutch and Harrigan and this makes him more dangerous. Brody is also a terrific actor and proves to be a good anchor for the film. He lends gravitas and has enough charisma to be believable as the unelected leader of this highly dangerous group made up of very different people.

There is actually a fantastic cast in Predators. It makes a huge difference because a good actor can lift the material up and make a character more memorable on the screen than they might have been on the page. Aside from Lance Henricksen there was no one to do this in the AvP movies. Predators, by way of contrast, has plenty of charisma among the cast and they all do some good work in this film. Walter Scoggins is sort of the comic relief character as the death row convict but he knows when to rein it in and doesn't unbalance the film.

Royce is a very reluctant hero in Predators and this makes him different from Dutch or Harrigan because their jobs (and the desire to gain revenge for their murdered friends) required them to be the hero and head towards danger. Royce, by contrast, feels like he doesn't owe anything to anyone and merely wants to survive. Royce doesn't care if the other characters die because they aren't his friends and he doesn't know them. He does though, in his gruff understated way, grow fond of Isabelle over the course of the film.

Brody's portrayal of Royce serves as a refreshing departure from the usual muscle-bound action hero archetype. Brody brings a nuanced intensity to the character, showcasing Royce as a cunning strategist forced into a reluctant leadership role. The film begins with Royce waking up to find himself hurtling through the air as if he's been thrown out of an aeroplane. This is an arresting and engaging start to the film. Despite much panic and confusion he safely parachutes into a jungle but has no memory of what happened to him or why he is here. Royce is armed though and soon begins to meet others who have had the same experience and now find themselves all stranded together.

Israel Defense Forces sniper Isabelle (Alice Braga), Revolutionary United Front officer Mombasa (Mahershalalhashbaz Ali), death row inmate Stans (Walton Goggins), katana wielding Yakuza enforcer Hanzo (Louis Ozawa Changchien), Mexican drug cartel enforcer Cuchillo (Danny Trejo), and Spetsnaz soldier Nikolai (Oleg Taktarov). They also pick up an unarmed and meek doctor named Edwin (Topher Grace) but have no idea whatsoever why he is here too. They have a common link in that they are all lethal assassins and killers but Edwin's presence is yet one more puzzle.

We quickly get a demonstration of how cunning Royce is because he outflanks Nikolai (who had been firing on him and Cuchillo) and surprises him. This disparate and bickering group begin to explore and look for a way out of the jungle but they can't seem to get their bearings from compass readings or the sun. Something is wrong - very wrong. When they reach higher ground they realise what the problem is. They see a sky that is clearly not of Earth. They are on an alien planet or moon. Royce soon begins to realise what the true nature of their predicament is. They have been specifically chosen because of their lethal talents so that they can be used to sharpen hunting skills. These deadly human killers have been transplanted to a Predator big game reserve and the hunt is about to begin.

Predators has a really good premise - so good in fact that it is impossible for the film to do this premise full justice. One problem is that alien jungle in the film is always quite clearly Hawaii. It would have been great if the more they explored the jungle the more weird, strange and alien it got but this never happens - presumably because they simply didn't have the budget. The freefall sequence at the start is an interesting way to begin and immediately captures your attention and the initial sequences with the characters exploring the jungle and becoming confused about where exactly they are build tension and intrigue. It's all very The Outer Limits and off kilter.

This is exactly what the AvP movies lacked - atmosphere and tension. Predators uses the original Predator as its primary touchstone and while it can never realistically match that film it does manage to capture fragments of that classic Predator residue. The concept of a group of international killers and soldiers with different weapons and skills being hunted by Predators sounds great but there is never quite enough of these characters actually being hunted. By introducing a bunch of Predators the creature loses a little bit of mystique too. What you really miss in this film is the simple but effective formula of a lone Predator lurking in the trees and shadows.

Considering they are supposed to be on a Predator game reserve there is often a distinct lack of Predator action in this film at times. Certainly compared to the second film at least. You only ever see a handful of Predators and they lack the spine ripping skull collecting mystique of earlier incarnations. They even introduce a plot thread where there is some sort of feud between two rival tribes of Predators and Royce tries to help one side in the hope of finding allies. Developments like this are questionable creative decisions. Just have a Classic Predator and make it a nasty mysterious creature who hunts humans. That's all you really need.

This film is much better cast than the 2018 film The Predator. Adrien Brody, as we've noted, is a surprisingly good lead and Alice Braga is also good as Isabelle. You actually believe that Braga is a sniper and not only is she a convincing action character she also has some chemistry with Brody. Walter Goggins and Topher Grace both make the most of their roles as the two radically different serial killers and bring some levity to the film without going over the top. Danny Trejo isn't in the film for long though and feels a trifle wasted. Louis Ozawa Changchien as the Yakuza enforcer doesn't say much but he does get to take on a Predator with his traditional Japanese katana sword in a well staged fight scene.

The characters in this film aren't fleshed out much but they don't really need to be. We get who they are and where they've come from and their interactions are interesting because, despite most of them being lone wolves, they've no choice but to work together. Compare this with 2018's The Predator - where the characters were so forgettable you barely noticed when they started getting killed off. What really helps in Predators too is that the characters are very distinctive and different. They all have their personalities and different costumes and weapons. Contrast this to Paul W. S Anderson's Alien vs Predator - where the characters were bland and in some cases too similar to even tell apart.

The tension and atmosphere - that sense of danger - of the first film (or even the second) is never quite replicated in Predators but Nimrod Antal does a decent enough job with what was clearly a limited budget. The jungle isn't as lush or foreboding as the one in the first film and some the digital matte effects look a bit anachronistic. This is a fairly stripped down film that never looks like it had a huge amount of money at its disposal. Not necessarily a bad thing but anyone looking for a big epic blockbuster here is likely to walk away disappointed.

Some of the action in Predators is good but it never has that visceral edge of the first two and is slick rather than exciting. The film is though very watchable. It draws you in and also holds up to further viewings. Predators is always interesting and generally entertaining and compelling. The inclusion of Predator dogs is certainly a questionable decision (it just seems out of character for the Predators to have pet hunting dogs!) and doesn't really work (unbelievably, the next Predator film in 2018 would actually double down on this idea too!) but there's enough good stuff in Predators to mitigate its flaws.

The score is pretty good and the characters encountering the strange alien sky is a good reveal. "We're going to need a new plan," drawls the understated Royce. The death of Danny Trejo's character is creepy and there are some decent moments of gore and Predator ripping action. Predators is a likeable film in that it doesn't have the biggest budget in the world but it is clearly doing its best to give you a good time.

It should be mentioned that Laurence Fishburne gives a highly eccentric performance as Noland, the soldier who has somehow survived on the moon and gone insane as a result. Fishburne is there to be Basil Exposition and explain the planet and the Predator feud to us and the main characters. Maybe necessary but clunky anyway. You never really believe that he could have survived alone for years on the planet killing Predators. Still, this character does serve a function because the characters go to a crashed ship he is holed up in and we essentially get some claustrophobic metallic spaceship style sequences when the Predators move in for the kill. The film probably needed this texture shift because the jungle scenes were becoming a trifle samey.

One obvious problem with Predators is that it doesn't really have an ending. When the film ends, Royce and Isabelle are still trapped on the game reserve. It feels like a bit of a cheat really - as if the writers went 'we'll just leave the film there and hope we get a sequel'. A spaceship used by the Predators to get on and off the moon has been alluded to throughout the film but we never actually get to see inside it. It would have been nice to see Royce and Isabelle make it to the ship at the end and at least that would have been a more satisfying ending.

One minor drawback of Predators is that some characters receive less development than desired. While the film endeavors to give each character their moment, the large ensemble cast leaves a few individuals in the periphery of the narrative, lacking the depth needed to fully connect with the audience. Another flaw in Predators is that the doctor Edwin is determined to kill everyone at the end but surely this would leave him alone with no protection on the planet? Maybe we are just meant to presume that Edwin is insane and thinks he can strike some sort of deal with the Predators because he believes he is like them. Edwin presumably wants to stay on the planet because there will be fresh humans parachuted in for him to kill. How would he even survive though? What would he eat?

Predators never quite cuts loose and becomes a thrill ride but it is very watchable and the night sequences in particular are well staged. The characters are good and the premise is always intriguing. Some of the Predator masks are a trifle on the silly side but - generally - this is a decent enough film and proved there was some life left in the Predator franchise. I would rank Predators below the first two films but it is still a fairly solid entry in this franchise.

Predators is nothing awe inspiring but it did help to take away the bad taste left by the AvP movies. The reputation of Predators was also boosted by the 2018 film film the Predator. I suspect a lot of people like me, despite not being wowed by the film in 2010, developed a new appreciation for Predators after The Predator came out. We looked back at Predators, watched it again, and realised it was a better film than we gave it credit for at the time. When you consider that Predators cost about the same amount of money to make as Aliens vs Predator: Requiem you realise that Robert Rodriguez and Nimrod Antal did a pretty good job because the difference between those two movies is night and day.

The reviews for Predators were what you could describe as mixed. It ended up with 65% on Rotten Tomatoes - which is respectable if not spectacular. Many critics felt it was perfectly fine for what it was and praised Antal for delivering a stylish looking film on a modest budget. Other critics though felt the movie was too in hock to the original Predator and came across as a diluted and lightweight reheated version of the 1987 film.

Curiously, a lot of critics seemed to aim a few barbs at Adrien Brody and didn't seem to think he made a very good action hero in Predators. I'd disagree with that myself but everyone is entitled to their view I suppose. A lot of critics felt there wasn't enough Predator action in the movie too - which is fair enough. The one thing everyone did agree on was that Predators was a vast improvement on the two AvP films we'd been served up since Predator 2.

Predators grossed around $130 million at the box-office. It wasn't a blockbuster but because it was produced on a modest budget the film was able to turn in a modest profit.

Predators evidently did not though quite do well enough to get a direct sequel so we'll never know if Royce and Isabelle got off that planet! Not that the writers of Predators didn't try. They pitched a sequel where Royce and Isabelle lead a resistance movement on the Predator game reserve and then manage to get onto a spaceship.

The idea was to do a sort of 'Die Hard on a Spaceship' type film with Royce and Isabelle battling Predators on the ship. There was then going to be a twist Planet of the Apes style ending where they make it to Earth but find it's now the future. Litvak and Finch also pitched an unrelated sequel where a Predator ship full of weird aliens crashes on Earth and the creatures get loose in a city. In the end Fox declined to move forward with any of these ideas because they had new plans of their own for the franchise.

THE PREDATOR (2018)

Fans of the Predator series were excited when it was announced in 2014 that Shane Black had signed to direct a fourth film in the franchise. Black said that he originally turned down the offer but was persuaded to do it when Fox promised him a generous budget which would allow him to make a Predator film full of 'spectacle'. Black played Hawkins in the original Predator and was now an established film director - in addition to being a veteran screenplay expert. Black had recently directed big movies like Iron Man 3 and was pretty A-list at the time - so it was something of a coup for the Predator franchise to get him. What could possibly go wrong?

The film would be co-written with Fred Dekker (of The Monster Squad and Night of the Creeps fame - Shane Black actually wrote The Monster Squad with Dekker *). Night of the Creeps is a cult 1986 low-budget sci-fi horror film written and directed by Dekker. Dekker must feature on any list of the unluckiest people in Hollywood. After Night of the Creeps and his affectionate horror spoof The Monster Squad he seemed to have a great future but the Robocop 3 debacle made him persona non grata and he was banished to television script editing. A shame really.

Night of the Creeps throws in every B-film horror/science fiction reference imaginable and like many eighties horror films has its tongue planted in cheek, riffing as it does on 1950s paranoia sci-fi and the conventions of the eighties college campus comedy film. It's like Night of the Living Dead, Dawn of the Dead, It Came from Outer Space and Invasion of the Body Snatchers all blended together with a John Hughes film and Revenge of the Nerds. What is most enjoyable about Night of the Creeps though is the presence of horror veteran Tom Atkins with his trademark mustache and craggy face. Atkins was/is an unconventional leading man best known for films like The Fog and Halloween III and his turn here as a sarcastic but heroic police detective must surely rank as the actor's finest hour. I'm not surprised that Atkins always names Night of the Creeps as his favourite film.

Shane Black told the media that his Predator film would not be a reboot but a sequel which explored the 'mythology' of the Predator universe. He said that one of his (slightly surprising) touchstones for the film would be Steven Spielberg's Close Encounters of the Third Kind. Black wanted his Predator movie to capture the 'wonder and mystery' of Close Encounters. The thought of Shane Black and Fred Dekker doing a Predator film almost sounded too good to be true. They do say though it's the hope that kills you.

Shane Black and the studio certainly talked a good game after announcing this film. The producer John Davis told the media that The Predator would set up two sequels which he hoped Shane Black would also direct. We were told that the script was 'amazing' and 'surprising'. The film was also allocated nearly double the budget of 2010's Predators - which clearly showed how much faith the studio had in Shane Black. As ever, there was talk of Arnold Schwarzenegger taking some sort of small role in the film but this never transpired. Schwarzenegger was going to show up as Dutch in a helicopter right at the end of the film. Schwarzenegger later said he turned down the offer because he didn't like the script for the movie and his role only amounted to a cameo.

The rapper '50 Cent' spoke about being in the film but this never happened either. Benicio del Toro was supposed to have the lead role in The Predator but he was too busy to do it in the end. That's a shame because Benicio del Toro would have brought some badly needed offbeat charisma to the film. Bradley Cooper, Ben Affleck, and James Franco are said to have passed on the lead role of Quinn. The UFC fighter Conor McGregor said in an interview that he also turned down a 'lead' role in The Predator because the money on offer was not very generous and he didn't feel like spending eight weeks in Canada because his girlfriend was pregnant.

In the end the lead role was played by Boyd Holbrook. Holbrook had many credits but was probably best known for his role as the villain in the Wolverine film Logan. Olivia Munn, who was cast as Dr Casey Brackett, also had many credits but was best known for playing Psylocke in one of the X-Men films. Trevante Rhodes, who was cast as Nebraska Williams, is an Award winning actor known for films like Moonlight. Keegan-Michael Key, cast as Coyle, also has a lot of credits but is perhaps best known for being part of the Key & Peele sketch comedy duo.

Thomas Jane was cast as Baxley (a nod to Craig no doubt). Back in the day, Jane was the lead in films like The Punisher and Deep Blue Sea. He never quite became a big star but he is a cultish sort of actor. He seemed to be making a lot of direct to video movies before being cast in The Predator. Sterling K. Brown, cast as Agent Will Traeger, was another versatile and experienced actor in the cast. Shortly before The Predator he had appeared in the popular Marvel film Black Panther. Jacob Tremblay was a Canadian child actor (he's obviously a teenager now at the time of writing) who had won numerous awards. He was cast as the son of Boyd Holbrook's character.

The Ecuadorian-American actor Augusto Aguilera was cast as the pilot Nettles and Yvonne Strahovski was cast as the wife of Holbrook's character Quinn. Strahovski is a familiar face through TV shows like Dexter and Chuck. These days she is best known as Serena Waterford in the dystopian drama The Handmaid's Tale.

Yvonne Strahovski is a bit wasted in The Predator and doesn't have much to do in the film. Alfie Allen, who plays the sniper Lynch, is best known for his role as Theon Greyjoy in Game of thrones. Jake Busey, in a nod to Predator 2, was cast as Sean Keyes - son of Peter. I don't have many positive things to say about The Predator but I'll give it credit for not pretending that Predator 2 doesn't exist!

The veteran actor Edward James Olmos - who many will know best for the brilliant reboot of Battlestar Galactica - was also cast too as a military officer named General Woodhurst in The Predator. His character was the boss of the government agent Will Traeger. In interviews during the production, Olmos talked about how 'funny' The Predator was as a movie and called it 'big' and 'crazy'. The word 'funny' probably should have set some sort of alarm bells ringing because while the Predator films all have a small degree of humour they are not comedies.

If you watch a Predator film there are plenty of things you expect and demand (gore, action, tension, scares, horror, guns! etc) but comedy is definitely not one of them. Maybe though this was something we should have seen coming. Shane Black is, a bit like James Gunn, known for his somewhat irreverent and offbeat approach to mainstream moviemaking. While this proved to be a strength on something like Iron Man 3 (not everyone loved this film but you can't deny that Black was able to give what could have been a very generic product some surprises and plenty of wit) it most assuredly did not prove to be a strength when it came to The Predator.

It was soon revealed that The Predator would be set in the present day in suburbia. While the concept of the Predator running around in suburbia was appealing at first glance there was an obvious problem which soon sprang to mind. The last Alien v Predator film was also set in an ordinary present day American backdrop. This meant that The Predator ran the risk of feeling generic and not doing anything new. The presumption was though that a smart man like Shane Black surely must have something clever up his sleeve to avoid this. Well, sadly, it turned out that there was nothing up Shane Black's sleeve at all. Fred Dekker was sleeveless too. The Predator is awash with baffling creative decisions and plot strands that go absolutely nowhere.

By now it was common to suggest that this franchise should try and do something different. Why not, for example, have a Predator story set in a different historical time period? Why does it always have to be the present day? Well, that would happen soon enough. There were behind the scenes problems on The Predator when Olivia Munn, one of the stars of the film, was furious when she found out that Shane Black's friend Steven Wilder Striegel had a scene in the film. Steven Wilder Striegel had been a registered felony sex offender since 2010, when he pleaded guilty to "enticing a minor by computer" after he attempted to lure a 14-year-old girl into a sexual relationship via email. He spent five months in jail.

Munn's complaints led to executives cutting Striegel's scene from the film. Munn said she found it - "Both surprising and unsettling that Shane Black, our director, did not share this information to the cast, crew, or Fox Studios prior to, during, or after production. However, I am relieved that when Fox finally did receive the information, the studio took appropriate action by deleting the scene featuring Wilder prior to release of the film." Black had to offer an apology for casting Steven Wilder Striegel in the film. Striegel's deleted scene was a cameo in which he played a jogger who (unsuccessfully) tries to chat up Olivia Munn's scientist character Dr Brackett.

The original story in The Predator had two 'emissionary' Predators coming to Earth to team up with humans to fight the giant 'Upgrade' Predator. Early photographs from the set featured two Predators in an armoured vehicle with the human characters. One of the 'fugitive' Predators, in the original script, had stolen the 'Ark' - a ship full of deadly Predator hybrid creatures (like Predator style spiders) which it didn't want the giant super Predator to use against humanity. The film, as originally shot, had the Ark captured by the military and taken to Area 51 - whereupon the creatures escape. The original version of The Predator sounds absolutely bonkers but - whether sadly or not - we would never get to see it for ourselves.

The film originally featured the 'Loonies' (the gang of human military misfits) fighting the hybrid Predator creatures. During the production there were actually leaked photographs of some of the death scenes of the characters. Though they didn't know it at the time the actors would have to come back and shoot completely different death scenes.

The special effects for these hybrid creatures were not quite completed when the film was screened for test audiences and the screenings did not go well at all. Test audiences found The Predator to be a complete misfire and this eventually prompted the studio to make some big changes.

The first cut of the film began with a block of text which explained that Project Stargazer had been set up to monitor Predator activity on Earth. The film's original ending had Quinn looking up at the sky after vanquishing the giant Predator in the forest and saying - "come and get us motherf******." Shane Black said that even the CGI which had been completed looked lousy in these hybrid sequences because they took place in broad daylight. Black and the studio decided the first cut wasn't scary at all because of all the daylight scenes. Basically, they felt the film was unreleasable in its present form.

"We were trying to cram a lot into a five pound bag," said Black. "We had a big appetite and wanted to do all of this stuff but to save some money, we needed to shoot during the day because it would be prohibitive during the night. I take this on me, but when I saw the footage that was shot during the day - which was the climax of the movie - the Predator just didn't look right. It just didn't look scary in the daytime. The we decided to streamline the plot and concentrate on the scarier elements that would let us do the reshoots at night. The difference is literally night and day."

The studio (and doubtless Shane Black) were also spooked by all the dismal test screenings. This resulted in around half of the film being completely reshot. Filming on The Predator took place in British Columbia from February to June 2017. The reshoots were done just over a year later in July 2018. What this all meant was that the emissionary Predators and hybrid creatures were jettisoned from the film. The character played by Edward James Olmos, who was evidently connected to this part of the plot, was also cut from the film.

While there have been cases where films underwent substantial reshoots but turned out fine (the Star Wars film Rogue One for example), The Predator was not one of them. Heaven knows how bad the original version of The Predator must have been if they thought that the actual film with all the reshoots was a big improvement! The mind boggles at how awful the first version must have been. What replaced all of the jettisoned material was a cobbled together third act in which the human characters are hunted by the lumbering Upgrade Predator in a forest at night. This third act was every bit as unexciting as that synopsis makes it sound.

Suffice to say then, a plot thread which at least sounded rather intriguing (Predators teaming up with humans) was replaced by something completely generic and forgettable. Given that the special effects were never completed and this film was not a big smash at the box-office, the chances of us ever getting see a cut of the original version of the film with the emissionary Predators would appear to close to zero. Whatever the original cut was about and whatever its shortcomings may have been, it is hard to imagine it could have been any worse than what we ended up with.

Curiously, two other endings were shot for The Predator but neither was used. In one, instead of the 'Predator killer suit', the pod reveals Ripley from the Alien series. Breanna Watkins played

Ripley - though you wouldn't have seen Ripley's face, only a name tag. In the other deleted scene, the pod was going to reveal a grown-up Newt from Aliens. Breanna Watkins (again) played Newt. These two sequences are rather bizarre but certainly interesting.

These aborted sequences were presumably meant to somehow link to Neill Blomkamp's planned Alien 5 - which would have ignored everything after Aliens and brought back Newt, Hicks, and Ripley (despite all three being killed off in Alien 3). As we know though, Blompkamp's Alien film never got made in the end. The release date for The Predator was changed three times before settling on September 2018. With all the publicity about the reshoots there was a sense that The Predator was a film in trouble by the time it finally arrived. Alas, all those fears turned out to be true.

REVIEW

The story begins with a U.S. Army Ranger sniper named Quinn McKenna (Holbrook) encountering a crashed Predator spaceship while on a jungle mission. He manages to capture some of the Predator's advanced technology and mails it to his home, fearing that the government will try to cover up the existence of extraterrestrial beings if he hands it over. That's very trusting of Quinn to think it will actually reach America! The Predator tech (a helmet and gauntlet) is unwrapped by Quinn's son Rory (Jacob Tremblay). Rory is a shy and bullied but highly intelligent kid who has a form of autism.

Meanwhile, a U.S government agency is aware of the Predators' existence and is actively studying them. Dr Casey Bracket (Olivia Munn), a biologist, is brought in by the authorities to examine a captured Predator. However, during the examination, the Predator awakens and escapes. Quinn has been questioned by the authorities and is now handcuffed and put on a bus - which is destined for a mental institution. The other detainees on the bus are an eccentric bunch who come to be unofficially known as the 'Loonies'. They are former Marine officer Nebraska Williams (Trevante Rhodes), Marine veteran Coyle (Keegan-Michael Key), expert sniper Lynch (Alfie Allen), Tourettes afflicted Marine veteran Baxley (Thomas Jane), and pilot Nettles (Augusto Aguilera).

When the 'Loonies' see the Predator which escaped from the government facility attacked by a much larger Predator they hijack the bus, team up with Dr Casey Bracket, and head for Quinn's house. It transpires that the Predators are seeking to extract human DNA and fear they must hurry up because climate change might finish off humanity sooner than we think. Not only do they have the giant super Predator to deal with but also government agent Will Traeger (Sterling K. Brown)...

The Predator begins reasonably well with an effective jungle sequence in which Quinn acquires the alien tech. The sequence where the Predator escapes from the government facility is also well staged and enjoyable. From here on in though the film goes downhill and never really recovers. The Predator feels like a movie that is always groping for a plot or story which it never actually manages to find. There is no real rhyme or reason to The Predator. It feels like watching a film that got lost in an editing room. It never fits together into any sort of coherent whole.

You have these various story threads set up but none of them actually go anywhere and by the time the picture reaches the third act it feels like it is on autopilot. The third act is such a painting by numbers yawnfest that it is hard to believe this is a Shane Black film. Out of the five stand alone Predator films, The Predator is by far the dullest to sit through. No matter how many times I've seen them, I can happily rewatch all of the Predator films - all except for The Predator. There is just something about this film that doesn't engage. It becomes a chore to sit through.

You can pinpoint where the film begins to display worrying signs - the first introduction of the 'Loonies' on the bus and the moment where Dr Brackett, initially a meek scientist, is suddenly jumping onto buses like Lara Croft in pursuit of the Predator. The tone of this movie is all over the place. It can't seem to decide what it is supposed to be. The Predator ultimately fails miserably to ever justify its existence as another entry in the Predator franchise. The Predator is a mess. There is no clarity of purpose or any clever idea or concept. It makes Predators look like a masterpiece in comparison.

It seems that The Predator got lost somewhere along the line with the reshoots and became a film that was impossible to salvage. The Predator is such a hollow and nothing sort of film that it barely feels like a movie at all. It's like watching a collection of scenes randomly strung together in no coherent order. It quickly dawns on the viewer that Boyd Holbrook's Quinn is a desperately dull leading character in The Predator. No one is ever going to replace Arnold Schwarzenegger as Dutch but Predator 2 managed to get around this by having the story anchored by the dependable Danny Glover - who was a strong screen presence in that film and a surprisingly effective action hero to boot.

Adrien Brody in Predators was an interesting lead because the actor was cast against type. The fact that Royce was also mysterious and fairly immoral at times (you genuinely got the impression that Royce would have killed all the other characters himself if he thought it was necessary to his own survival) gave the character some depth and even a bit of unpredictability. Quinn, by way of contrast, is just bland. He has no character development or personality at all. He is instantly forgettable. Quinn is an absolute blank of a character. He is generic and boring. Holbrook just doesn't have the commanding screen presence of an Arnie or Danny Glover. He's more of a supporting actor than leading man.

The same can be said of the 'Loonies' who serve as the heroes in The Predator. You are unlikely to remember any of the names of these pointless and underfleshed characters after you've watched the film. The introduction of these characters on the bus is an early warning for what will follow. Shane Black clearly wants us to find these characters hilarious, crazy, and memorable. But we don't at all and their shtick soon grows tiresome. The heart sinks somewhat during the bus scene at the thought of now having to spend an entire film with these characters. None of them are fleshed out and they don't really have much personality - despite all the foul-mouthed humour and constant jokes.

There's an air of desperation about the jokes and performances in The Predator. The cast are trying to make this work but the script and material is a thin watery soup which has nothing for them to get their teeth into. Even the usually reliable Thomas Jane can't keep his head above water in The Predator with his Tourettes character Baxley - who is meant to be funny. You probably would have been better off casting Jane as the lead and getting rid of most of the supporting characters. At least we know Jane has some charisma from past work.

The problem is that the script and these characters are never as funny as Black clearly intended them to be and so both the 'Loonies' and the endless deluge of jokes become annoying and tiresome very fast. These jokes frequently land with a thud. It's like the moment early on when they go down into the government facility and a worker does a spooky voice and a line from the Haunted Mansion Disney theme park attraction as a gag. Did this moment really need a joke? The joke isn't even funny. Why is everyone constantly in quip mode in a Predator film?

The problem with having characters constantly dispensing jokes is that it dissipates the tension. The characters in the first Predator film are strictly business once the danger and tension arrives. The characters in this film just stay goofy and in quip mode whatever is happening. Shane Black said he wanted the heroes in the film not to be stoic super soldiers but misfits and outsiders. He said he was inspired by Butch Cassidy & the Sundance Kid - where the characters use gallows humour and quips in difficult situations. While this all sounds reasonable on paper it simply doesn't work in the actual film. The characters in

The Predator are annoying - to the point where you don't actually care when any of them get killed.

Take Predator 2 by way of contrast. Bill Paxton's character Jerry Lambert in that film is a quip dispensing motormouth. But he's the ONLY character like this so he's a contrast to everyone else and has his own distinct personality. Imagine if EVERY single character in Predator 2 was like Jerry Lambert. It would be insufferable wouldn't it? Well, that's The Predator problem in a nutshell. Every male character in the film is a smartass comedian. They all become wearing long before the film has ended. And it isn't as if Jerry Lambert was in quip mode all the time. He's was all business when the Predator threatened the subway train.

Compare the deaths in (the unfairly maligned) Predator 2 also to The Predator. Jerrry Lambert goes out in the tense subway scene. Peter Keyes is cut in half by a Predator frisbee in the meat warehouse. King Willie loses his head in a rain puddled alley. These deaths are memorable. Can you even remember any of the deaths of the main characters in The Predator? It's a shame really that Edward James Olmos was cut from the film because he might have provided some of the gravitas and screen presence completely lacking in the main characters.

Sterling K. Brown as the nominal baddie Will Traeger is another character in the film that you'll struggle to remember afterwards. His main character trait is that he likes gum - which will give you some idea of the script. The special effects in the opening Predator crash sequence are decent but the sequence where the Predator is running away from the 'Looney' bus early on is rather risible because the Predator is too heavy and clunky and can clearly not run very fast at all. Predators are supposed to be agile and fast - not big clanking lunks who can barely run.

The film has many questionable and, at times, baffling creative decisions. Like the use of Predator Hounds - something we've already seen in Predators. One of the hounds is domesticated after suffering a head injury and used by the human characters to their advantage. These hounds aren't done especially well by the special-effects department and one tends to feel that it wouldn't have been a great loss if they'd been jettisoned altogether. The Predator Hound is sort of used for comic relief - only it isn't funny.

The Upgrade Predator is also fairly forgettable and doesn't bring much that is new to the table. This Predator is depicted by CGI and so doesn't have much personality. It never wears a mask either and the Predators tend to lose some mystery and mystique if they never wear their helmets. This Predator looks ridiculous. It looks more like a poorly designed generic monster than the classic Predator of old. Beside being really tall, this Predator is rather dull all things considered.

Being bigger than the other Predators is not exactly a brilliant concept! One rather misses the concept of a lone Classic Predator hunting unsuspecting humans from the shadows - a concept we hadn't actually seen since Predator 2. The Upgrade Predator has none of the mystique and menace of the Predators in the first two movies and because we can always see this Predator it comes across as a big boring monster rather than the Classic Predator of old. The Predator does at least have some gore and violence but there are few moments that really stand out in the film or stick in the memory.

The reshoots (it's a shame that we lost an APC action sequence in the cuts) obviously didn't help the narrative coherence and as a consequence of this the motivations of the characters (and indeed the Predators) are never entirely clear at the best of times. Why would the Predators be interested in human DNA? They are much stronger than us and much more advanced than us. The Predator somehow manages to be feel both plotless and empty but convoluted and overstuffed both at the same time - which is remarkable when you think about it.

Jacob Tremblay gives a sincere performance as the sensitive Rory but his scenes (like Rory being bullied or wandering around at

Halloween with the Predator mask on and accidentally killing someone!) often feel like they belong in another movie. Why is Quinn sending potentially dangerous alien tech to his house knowing that his son could injure himself or kill someone with it? Rory is seen as the next stage in evolution (or something) by the evil Predator because of his autism. The kid genius is a rather tired trope in sci-fi and action adventure films.

Olivia Munn as Casey also comes out of The Predator, or this cut at any rate, as a vague and generic character. By the end of the film we feel like we still barely know her and the script often requires her to perform stunts and action scenes which feel improbable. Quinn has some improbable action scenes too but we can suspend disbelief a trifle more easily because he's a highly trained army veteran. The ordinary present day locations in The Predator feel dull and generic and don't work as a backdrop to a Predator movie. This is not being wise after the event either because we already knew this from bitter experience. Did Shane Black not watch AvP: Requiem?

The jungle in the first Predator movie was scary and foreboding. The near future lawless Los Angeles depicted in the second movie was also scary and intimidating. The ordinary backdrops in The Predator are simply dull and boring. The third act of the movie brings all the characters together into a forest - where they are picked off by the Upgrade Predator. This pine forest is not a tremendously exciting location and the darkness and incoherent action direction often makes it difficult to even see what is happening. This was all, as we have noted, part of the reshoots and boy does it show. It is a lazy and slapdash climax for the film. The death of Traeger in particular is bizarre and confusing.

The sequence where Quinn, Nebraska, and Nettles jump on the Predator ship is especially ludicrous and tiresome. Nebraska causes the ship to crash by throwing himself into the turbine. Would an advanced alien spaceship really be disabled so easily? You'd think the Predators, who are so advanced they can travel across space to other planets, would have designed their ships so that such things were not possible! Rory has been captured by the Predator as a hybrid subject because of his autism. This rather goes against the Predator code because in the previous films they would not attack someone who was no threat to them - like a child. The big super Predator though clearly doesn't abide by any Predator code. This creature is such a stupid idea.

It's as if they had a brainstorming session to knock ideas around and someone said - Why don't we make the Predator twice as big as the other Predators? It'll be like the Andre the Giant of Predators! Amazingly, this was deemed a good idea and it went in the film. The Upgrade Predator, despite being impervious to weapons throughout the film, is eventually killed by Quinn and Casey on top of a cliff. The Upgrade Predator has numerous chances to kill Quinn but decides to throw him around like a WWF wrestler instead.

The final scene, where a 'Predator Killer' suit is deployed is yet another baffling creative decision in a film already festooned with baffling creative decisions. This final scene is beyond awful. Though this scene threatens some sort of direct sequel, mercifully, this did not transpire. The team who made The Predator plainly did not have enough good ideas for one film let alone a sequel. The main problems with The Predator are many and varied. For one thing there are too many characters and they all just jumble into one another in the end and have no distinct personality. None of the characters are given enough room to shine or develop.

Even the lead character Quinn doesn't feel that different from the other 'Loonies' and so never really stands out as a charismatic leader in the way that Dutch and Harrigan and even Royce did. The characters in the film are hastily introduced to us and feel shallow and undercooked. We don't really care about any of these people. Who these people are and what motivates them in the film is vague to say the least. The comedy elements in the film don't work. There are some comic lines and moments in the original Predator (the jokes by Hawkins for example) and even

Predators has some deadpan levity thanks to Topher Grace and Walter Scoggins but these moments are generally few and far between.

Predator films are not meant to be funny. There is nothing in this franchise that makes us expect or want a comedic approach. Shane Black is determined to make us laugh in The Predator though. He wants us to find this film witty and funny. But it just isn't. The Predator is not a witty film at all and the comic moments fall flat. Take the moment where Dr Brackett wakes up in bed and the 'Loonies' are all standing around her - having placed a bet on whether or not she will pick up a shotgun in alarm when she wakes. This scene is not funny at all and even comes across as a bit distasteful. And yet, Shane Black probably thought it was hilarious when he was writing it. He probably thought this would get a big laugh.

Another problem with The Predator is that the film is never very exciting. The action in the film is never that great. It's fun when the Predator escapes from the government facility but this sequence aside there is nothing in The Predator that lingers in the memory. During the production of this film we assumed that Shane Black would have some clever ideas and twists up his sleeve but it turned out that he didn't. Once the Predator hybrids and 'friendly' Predators subplot was dumped from the movie, there was plainly no plan B so we just ended up with these annoying and forgettable characters being bumped off in the woods in the dark. This section of The Predator is like watching an expensive fan film. It is very mediocre and lazy.

Another problem with The Predator is that the giant Upgrade Predator has no mystique because it never wears a helmet. The scene where the Predator uses a translator to talk to the humans and tells them to run is especially ludicrous and also destroys the mystique of the Predator. The Predator (quite rightly) got disastrous reviews and was left with a Rotten Tomatoes score of 34%. Fred Dekker had this to say of the (understandable) fan backlash to this terrible film - "We live in a culture that's so cacophonous we sometimes cling to our opinions as our only voice in the din. Or we're so married to our childhood memories of things we love that when the formula is contradicted, some feel betrayed by any attempt to take a different approach. In all candour, I have lots of issues with the movie (I also hate the super-suit ending!), but I spent three years on it and to have it trashed by toxic fans who don't have the first clue how hard it is to get anything on the screen, well...that hurts."

Critics of The Predator were not 'toxic' fans. They simply hated the movie! No one went into this film wanting it to be bad or having any particular axe to grind. We just wanted a good Predator film and - sadly - we didn't get one. Out of the four Predator films (let's leave the AvP films out of this) made at the time, The Predator was by some considerable distance the worst. The Predator was not, contrary to some reports, a box office dud. It made $160 million - which was not a disaster but not spectacular either. The chances of another Predator film in the near future were certainly not great though - or so it seemed at the time.

The Predator was certainly a frustrating wasted opportunity because it was allocated a larger than usual budget and Shane Black seemed as good a choice as anyone at the time to bring the franchise back to its early salad days. The film that emerged though was hobbled by the reshoots and had a lot of the hallmarks of studio interference. A lot of Predator fans were wary of the initial reports that the film would feature hybrid creatures and 'friendly' Predators in combat fatigues but, in hindsight, it's a shame that original version of the movie didn't make it to the screen because it couldn't have been any worse than what we ended up with.

The Predator is a truly terrible film. It barely feels like a movie at all with the confused story and tone, undercooked characters, and thrown together at the last minute third act. What ended up on the screen wasn't much of an improvement on AvP: Requiem - and that's an incredible thing to say of an $80 million Predator film with Shane Black at the helm! The annoying thing about all of this is that The Predator got quite a bit of buzz when it first announced. What with the participation of Shane Black and a generous budget we were hopeful that The Predator might put this franchise back in the premier league and give us a highly memorable film. None of this happened in the end.

With the muddled script and reshoots the film was torpedoed before it even came out. Things certainly looked bleak for the Predator franchise after this fiasco but, amazingly, another Predator film was already in the pipeline. Would it be any good though? The last thing the Predator franchise needed was two bad movies in quick succession.

* The Monster Squad is a cult 1987 comedy horror adventure film directed by Fred Dekker. Dekker also wrote the screenplay with Shane Black. The story begins with a Transylvania prologue set in 1887. At a spooky castle, Dr Van Helsing (Jack Gwillim) attempts to banish Count Dracula (Duncan Regehr) into limbo on the "day of balance" between good and evil. This is only possible once every century and an indestructible shimmering green amulet of concentrated good must be at hand. Are you following this so far? Anyway, Van Helsing "blew it" (as the irreverent text scroll at the start of the film tells us) and Dracula resurfaces one hundred years later in 1987. The amulet was hidden far away in a small American town by Van Helsing's associates and the Count arrives to claim it and so plunge the world into darkness. To this end he puts together a team of classic Universal studio monsters to help him. Frankenstein's Monster (Tom Noonan), The Mummy (Michael MacKay), The Gill-Man aka Creature from the Black Lagoon (Tom Woodruff Jr), and The Wolf Man (Carl Thibault). The only thing that stands in their way is a bunch of plucky monster obsessed kids with a treehouse who call themselves The Monster Squad. Let battle commence.

This film seemed to slip through a portal into limbo itself but seems to be getting the love it deserves now. What a fun idea to use the classic Universal monsters and put them into a contemporary setting. Was this the first time they had all appeared together? I think it might have been. Stan Winston's enjoyable re imagining of the iconic monsters (love his Gill-Man, surely the inspiration for his Predator alien?) is wonderful. The Monster Squad takes a while to get going but once it does it's about as much fun as you have any right to expect a film to be. This is often compared to The Goonies but I don't really see a huge comparison myself apart from both pictures revolving around a bunch of kids. The Goonies is Spielberg assembly line stuff for children whereas The Monster Squad has a sharp script by Shane Black that has plenty for adults.

This is a strange film in many ways as children would clearly get a big kick out of it but it sometimes ventures into areas you wouldn't expect. Dracula calls a little girl a "bitch", the little girl calls her friends "chickens***s", there's a very funny and at times risque subplot about The Monster Squad trying to find a female virgin to read the monster banishing incantation from Van Helsing's diary. The sequence where The Wolf Man transforms in the back of an ambulance is pretty frightening. Note the scene too where the "Scary Old German Man" (charmingly played by Leonardo Cimino), who the Monster Squad befriend because he can translate Van Helsing's diary for them, is told that he seems to know a lot about monsters by one of the kids. "Now that you mention it, I suppose I do," he reflects and as he closes the door we see a Nazi concentration camp prisoner tattoo on his arm.

It always helps the film a lot that the children playing The Monster Squad are all likeable and handle the comedy with a decent amount of deftness. Andre Gower (looking uncannily like a young Tom Atkins) is the club leader Sean and Roddy Kiger is his best friend Patrick. Brent Chalem (who sadly died when he was only 22) is the "fat kid" Horace and has a great arc in the film - and also the most famous line in The Monster Squad when he comes up with a unique way to subdue The Wolf Man. Love the bit where Horace improvises and attacks Dracula with a slice of pizza because of the garlic. Ryan Lambert is Rudy, a slightly older kid who joins the team and is sort of like the cool one. He wears a leather jacket and sunglasses. He's the Fonz of the team if you will. Rudy has a memorable scene where he takes on three vampiric schoolgirls that Dracula has taken over. "Where the hell am I supposed to find silver bullets? K-Mart?" snaps Rudy when they discuss how to kill a werewolf.

By the way, as werewolves can only be killed by silver bullets, ever wondered what would happen if you blew up The Wolf Man with dynamite? There's a fun moment in the film where we find out. Ashley Bank is funny as Sean's younger sister Phoebe and is given some amusing lines by the script. I like the team's dog too and he features in a treehouse joke that made me laugh more than any other single moment in the film. The script is very Shane Black and you find yourself enjoying even the smallest dialogue moments. A bit near the start where Sean and Patrick have been hauled into the headmaster's office at school because they were overheard saying that one of their teachers had a head like a cat. Patrick tries to distance himself from the accusation and declares that he would never compare a teacher's head to that of a cat. "I mean, HOW rude!" he adds by way of an exclamation mark.

The monsters themselves are well cast with Tom Noonan making the most of the more sympathetic role of Frankenstein's Monster and Canadian actor Duncan Regehr (who I recognised from some episodes of Star Trek) enjoying himself as a suave sneering Dracula. "Meeting adjourned," says Drac when he blows their clubhouse up. The Mummy features in an inventive car chase sequence and I suppose the only complaint one could have with the monsters is that The Gill-Man only has a couple of scenes. He's makes a nice entrance though when Count Dracula summons him from a fog bound lake. This is not one of those films either where the adults are too stupid to notice what is going on for the entire film and Stephen Macht as Sean's police detective dad also becomes mixed up in the mayhem. I like the scenes where Macht and Sean sit on the roof of their house with binoculars to watch a drive-through horror film playing in the valley below. Sure, The Monster Squad is contrived and silly but I would defy anyone not to have a good time watching this film. The 'thumbs-up' exchange near the end must surely be one of the greatest moments in cinema history. Even the somewhat dated special effects are a lot of fun. Richard Edlund's spinning limbo vortex. Anyway, it boggles my mind that the men behind The Monster Club and Night of the Creeps could make a film as bad as The Predator!

PREY (2022)

Prey began as an idea that Dan Trachtenberg and the writer Patrick Aison had several years ago. Trachtenberg was the director of the mystery thriller 10 Cloverfield Lane. 10 Cloverfield Lane is a good tense thriller with some fine performances. Trachtenberg has also directed on the television shows The Boys and Black Mirror. Trachtenberg had an idea for a back to basics Predator film which would feature a Comanche warrior - in this case a young Comanche woman who has to prove herself in a male dominated tribe where the men do the hunting. One of the main inspirations for Trachtenberg was the character of Billy from the original Predator. Trachtenberg loved this Native American character in the first film. Trivia - at an early stage of the script for the first Predator film, Billy was going to be the main character at one point.

Another thing that Trachtenberg wanted to do was to get back to the 'lone jungle hunter' simplicity of the first film - though in this case it would be a Great Plains hunter. That was welcome news because the previous Predator film, as we just noted, had strayed from this formula and fallen flat on its face. Trachtenberg said that the Comanche were always villains or sidekicks in old Hollywood films and wanted them to be the heroes for a change. Trachtenberg enlisted two Comanche women – Juanita Pahdopony and Jhane Myers - to help make the script more realistic and produce the film respectively. 20th Century Fox really liked Trachtenberg's concept but there was only one problem. At the time they were still making The Predator. They asked Trachtenberg to continue to work on the story for his proposed film until Shane Black had finished his own Predator movie.

As a consequence of this Trachtenberg's film went on the back burner for a time. He actually considered making it as a non Predator film at one point but - thankfully - this obviously didn't transpire in the end. After the Disney company acquired Fox, Trachtenberg feared they would no longer be interested in a new Predator film but this wasn't the case. It was the Fox production president Emma Watts who decided to fastrack the film. Trachtenberg had a clever pitch in that he told the studio that even though they were already making a Predator movie there was no reason why they couldn't do a completely different Predator movie too in the same way that different Star Wars projects can happen at the same time.

What appealed to the studio was that this new Predator film was something completely different. They also obviously liked the fact that Trachtenberg's treatment didn't sound as if it would cost an awful lot of money to produce. They wouldn't need any elaborate sets or many special effects. It was a very stripped down Predator film - not unlike the original. Prey was (appropriately enough for a Predator film) something of a cloaked stealth project at first and shrouded in secrecy. For quite a while it went under the title Skulls but this was obviously changed to Prey in the end. It would be the first Predator film not to actually use 'Predator' (or a slight variation) in the title.

Casting for Prey took place early in 2020. The wonderfully named Amber Midthunder was cast as the lead character Naru. Midthunder, despite only being in her mid-twenties, was something of an acting veteran - her first credit being as a child actor in 2001. She was probably best known for her role as Kerry Loudermilk in the dark superhero show Legion. Amber Midthunder said she was always wary of taking indigenous roles because she didn't think the representation of Native people in film and television was very good. She felt that Prey was different though and was excited to play Naru. Midthunder felt that Prey could be a very good film if it was done right.

Dakota Beavers was cast as Naru's brother Taabe. Beavers had never acted before when he got this part. At the time he was singing in bars at night and working in TJ Maxx during the day. Dan Trachtenberg said he likes to think that Billy from the original Predator is the reincarnated spirit of Taabe. Michelle Thrush was cast as Naru's mother in the film. Michelle Thrush is a Canadian First Nations activist and actor. She has been in many things - including Fargo, Northern Exposure, and Blackstone. Raphael Adolini, the Italian translator in the film played by Bennett Taylor, is the name of a character from the comic book Predator: 1718.

6'8 tall actor and former basketball player Dane DiLiegro was cast as the Predator in the movie - which was called the 'Feral Predator' by the crew. DiLiegro was cast because, while obviously incredibly tall, he was also slim and agile. They didn't want the Predator in the film to come across as some big lumbering hulk who could barely move. Because the film is set in 1719, this Predator has more basic and primitive versions of the weapons the Predators use in the later films - although the creature is no less deadly.

There are some nice touches in the film - like the way the Predator's cloaking technology isn't quite as smooth as the later Predators. You could say that if the later Predators are Blu-ray, this Predator is VHS! The Feral Predator doesn't have the familiar metallic Predator helmet and instead wears an alien skull as a mask. This Predator doesn't have a plasma shoulder cannon as Trachtenberg felt that would make the creature too overpowered - given that the human foes in this movie don't have modern guns. The Predator in Prey has a bolt gun instead of the shoulder cannon.

Not to say this alien isn't armed to the teeth though. He can deploy remote mines, has a shield which can be turned into a weapon, and even seems to have a net that is even more deadly than the one used in Predator 2. Around twenty designs were rejected before they settled on the look of the Feral Predator. Six Predator suits were made for Dane DiLiegro in order to cope with the wear and tear of shooting. Dan Trachtenberg said that Predator: Hunting Grounds was an influence on the way the Predator can traverse its environment in the film. Predator: Hunting Grounds is a multiplayer first-person shooter game developed by IllFonic and published by Sony Interactive Entertainment. It was released in 2020 for PlayStation 4 and Microsoft Windows.

Sarii, Naru's dog companion, was played by a Carolina dog named Coco who was acquired and trained specifically for the film. Prey is actually similar in concept to a 2019 short film called Warrior: Predator by Chris .R. Notarile. Prey was certainly in development before that film came out though. The flintlock pistol in Prey is obviously a nod to the end of Predator 2. This pistol also featured in the 1996 comic Predator; 1718. The end credits of Prey feature cave paintings - the last of which shows a Predator ship arriving at Naru's village. This is obviously an indication that the Predators haven't finished with Naru yet. They now consider her to be a worthy foe.

Prey was shot in Calgary, Alberta, Canada, in 2021. Stoney Nakoda First Nation land was used for much of the shoot. Amber Midthunder is part Nakoda. In November it was announced that the film would be called Prey and be released on Hulu as a streaming product. The budget was $65 million - which was smaller than The Predator's budget but nothing to sneeze at. The cast underwent weapons training before production began. Amber Midthunder spent a lot of time learning how to throw her character's axe in particular. The sign language the Comanche use in the film was worked out by the actors.

The original plan was for the characters to speak Comanche at the start and then have the camera pan in and out to signify that we are hearing Comanche translated into English. This device was used in The Hunt for Red October to explain why a Soviet submarine crew are speaking English. In the end though the characters in Prey simply speak English with no explanation. The cast later dubbed the film into Comanche so that you had a choice of which version you wanted. Naru refers to the Predator as a Mupitsi in the film. This word derives from a Comanche story about a cave dwelling demon that parents would tell obstreperous kids about to make them behave.

Filming wrapped on Prey in September 2021. There was quite an extensive post-production because many of the animals in the film had to be added through CGI. There were a few CG tweaks to the Predator in the film too. Some shots of the Predator in the film are purely CG - like the moments where you see the Predator jumping from tree to tree. Shots like these are obviously impossible to do with a stuntman in a Predator suit. It just wouldn't look good enough.

Prey is the first Predator sequel which didn't have to endure rather tiresome speculation over whether or not Arnold Schwarzenegger would be in it or make a cameo. It would obviously be a bit difficult for Dutch Schaefer to turn up in 1719! It is probably fair to say that Predator fans didn't know quite what to make of Prey before it came out. The film was certainly going to be a departure from the other films in the franchise.

Some liked the idea of a Predator film set in 1719 and some didn't. This would also be the first Predator film with a female lead - which unavoidably and depressingly led to some silly clickbait YouTube videos complaining that Prey was further evidence of how everything in Hollywood was too 'woke' these days.

A female lead in a Predator film was actually long overdue. If they'd made a third Predator film in the mid 1990s they could have had Geena Davis or Jamie Lee Curtis or someone like that going up against the Predator. Who wouldn't have wanted to see that? Prey would also have the first female composer too in Sarah Schachner. Schachner was especially known for her work on video games. It was certainly a nice surprise to get another Predator film again so soon but could Prey banish the sour taste left by The Predator or would it be another disappointment?

REVIEW

Prey concerns Naru, a young Comanche woman in 1719. Naru wants to be a warrior and hunter like her brother Taabe but her designated role is that of healer. The men in the tribe don't take the idea of a female hunter very seriously and Naru is basically told to stick to being a healer in the village and to leave all the hunting to the men. Naru is very frustrated by this and rebels against the conventions of the tribe. While on her own out in the wilderness, Naru sees strange lights in the sky which takes to be a Thunderbird. The thunderbird is a legendary creature in particular North American indigenous peoples' history and culture. It is considered a supernatural being of power and strength. Naru believes this is a sign that she is ready to be a hunter.

The tribe is concerned with the presence of a lion but Naru gradually becomes aware of a bigger threat - something a lot mysterious than a lion and even more dangerous too. She finds huge footprints and hears strange noises. The Predator is not the only thing Naru has to contend with either. There are also French trappers - who capture Naru and have plans to capture the 'Mupitsib' too. Good luck with that one French trappers! The Predator soon begins to target the humans in the area. It will be up to Naru and her brother Taabe to somehow find a way to vanquish this deadly and dogged beast.

Thankfully, Prey is a vast improvement on The Predator. A lot was riding on Prey but it mostly delivers the goods and is arguably the best Predator film since the original.

For many years now fans (or some of them anyway) have proposed that they should do a Predator film set in the past.

There are endless possibilities. A Predator hunting medieval knights or World War 2 soldiers. A Predator hunting Roman Centurions. And so on. Prey is the first film to do something like this and it works well once the movie gets goiing. It's refreshing to have a Predator film that isn't set in the present day yet again. Prey is not perfect but it feels novel and fresh because it is at least trying something new. You aren't just getting the same thing again.

What is nice too is that, after the convoluted nature of The Predator's plot, plus its large gallery of annoying characters, Prey feels very stripped down and is basically Naru and Taabe versus the Predator when you boil it down. Much was made of the fact that Prey sought to go back to the roots of the original film and have a human character relying on their wits to defeat the Predator in a primitive natural location. This is - happily - what you get in Prey.

All the other sequels sort of had a gimmick. The gimmick in Predator 2 is that the Predator was hunting in a city. The gimmick in Predators is that the characters were trapped on a Predator big game reserve. The gimmick in The Predator is that, well, I've no idea what the gimmick in The Predator was. Maybe the gimmick in that film was that the Predator is now a giant? I don't think anyone has ever actually worked out what the point of anything in The Predator was. The gimmick in Prey is that the film is set a long time in the past. It's a good gimmick though and gives us something new.

Prey is rather slow to get going - although there is plenty of atmosphere as Naru begins to suspect that there is something rather dangerous lurking in the Great Plains. The film is quite bold in that dialogue is very minimal at times and the story is often presented in a purely visual way. There's a bit of Dancing with Wolves here before the Predator action kicks in. Trachtenberg said he was inspired by films like Mad Max 2 (aka The Road Warrior) and Gravity - where the action often tells the story rather than reams of dialogue. The slow pacing at the start and some murky night scenes where it is hard to see anything make Prey quite difficult to get into at first but it soon becomes more compelling as it goes on and Naru is a likeable hero who is easy to root for.

At a leanish 99 minutes, Prey never threatens to outstay its welcome either - which is nice. Nitpickers were quick to point out that 5'5, 120 pound Amber Midthunder would be highly unlikely to be able to take down a Predator in reality but then so would Arnold Schwarzenegger, Danny Glover, Adrien Brody and Boyd Holbrook! It's only a film - not reality! And it's not as if Naru gets into a fistfight with the Predator or takes it out with a karate chop. She does actually use her wits and the environment to her advantage.

At one point we think Naru is going to use mud like Dutch in the first film to hide from the Predator but the film undercuts this assumption. Prey is smart in the way that it anticipates and subverts our expectations. Nara uses medicinal herbs to lower her body temperature (and thus hide from the Predator) - which is a clever idea. Another clever thing about the film is that the Predator doesn't initially see Naru as a threat or target. Naru only becomes a target when she earns respect through her bravery and fortitude.

There are a few too many animals being slaughtered in this film for my tastes but that's just me. I dislike animals being killed in films - even CGI animals! The fight between the bear and the Predator is well done - even if the bear is clearly not real. It's a clever way to show the brute strength of a Predator. This is not a lavish film in terms of special effects but it doesn't matter because the Predator design is well done and the locations are the real star. There are some terrific widescreen shots in this film. The burnt glade and smoke effects create some striking visual images in the film. It's a shame really that this film wasn't able to enjoy a traditional cinema release because it deserved to be seen on a big screen.

One of the great things about Prey is that the Predator in the film is nasty and vicious. This Predator is much more sinister and menacing than the ridiculous giant sized Predator in the last film. There is plenty of gore when the Predator takes on Comanche warriors and the film's finest hour comes when the creature battles a group of French trappers. Some of the new gadgets for the Predator are enjoyably inventive and it's great to see the creature use stealth and wits - in addition to some good old fashioned brute force. The net this Predator uses is so powerful it literally reduces one of the trappers to liquid!

The shots of the Predator jumping from tree to tree are also very well done. This conveys that the Predator is agile and able to move quickly. He's like a gymnast. As we've noted in some of the previous chapters, when the Predator seems too lumbering and slow it takes us out of the film because we are suddenly aware it's an actor in a suit. You have to use the creature sparingly and then make it fast and lethal when you do show the beast. They certainly do this in Prey to good effect. Naru becomes quite ruthless in the film too in order to survive, even using one of the trappers as bait.

The simplicity of Prey works to its advantage so it becomes a gripping story about survival and is short of subplots or tiresome attempts to explore the Predator mythology or change the modus operandi of these iconic fictional alien hunters. The fact that the film isn't deluged with supporting characters either is also a plus and allows Midthunder to shine in a fairly central spotlight. What is nice about the film too is that Naru has an arc and grows in confidence through the film. She begins the story as a young woman frustrated by the role assigned to her in this little society and ends the film as a mighty warrior who is sure to inspire many stories and legends.

An interesting and salient thing to note about Prey is that there are scenes of the Predator in daylight and they look fine. Shane Black said they dumped the third act of The Predator because they couldn't make day scenes with the Predator and other monsters work. Prey has no such problems. It still retains its mystique and primal alien quality - even in daylight. The alien in Prey seems more animal like than the Predators in the other films. It feels more primitive - which is keeping with the fact that this film is set hundreds of years ago. The alien in Prey is a very stripped down Predator with none of the high-tech armour we tend to associate with this hunter.

One of the keys to the success of Prey is that it harkens back to the original (and Predator 2) in that we have a lone Predator who is kept in the shadows for a while. The Predator in Prey is introduced very slowly - a tactic that works (just as it did in the original film). Predators and The Predator both tried to up the ante by introducing more Predators and suggesting there were different Predator factions who were at odds with one another. It is questionable whether or not any of this worked.

The films in this franchise work best when you have a solitary Predator hunting human characters. Once you deviate from that or try and change the Predator too much you run the risk of diluting the character. A lone Predator who is mysterious and deadly is far more novel and effective than a film with ten Predators who are constantly taking their masks off and killing one another.

Prey isn't perfect. It takes a while to get going and it is difficult to see what is going on in some of the early night scenes. This probably won't be everyone's cup of tea but if you are ready for something a bit different in the Predator franchise then Prey is a terrific film once it gets going. The best thing about Prey is that it finally allows the Predator franchise to stretch its legs and become a true anthology. Having the Predator movies constantly set on present day Earth was a blind alley that got old fast. To shake things up we needed some Predator films set in the past or the future or even outer space (Predators was obviously set on an alien world but that doesn't really count because the characters spent the film in a very Earth type jungle).

Prey is the first film to take up the challenge of doing a historical Predator story and it mostly succeeds in what it sets out to do. Prey is a vastly superior film to The Predator and showed there was still plenty of life in this franchise. What Prey illustrates is that Predator movies work best when they keep things simple. 2010's Predators had a raft of different Predators in the film involved in some sort of blood feud. The thing is though we didn't really care about this vague subplot. By having more than one Predator this diluted the creature and meant there was a lack of what should be the most basic concept of any Predator movie - the Predator actually hunting humans!

Another problem the Predator sequels have fallen into is having too many one-dimensional characters crammed into the film. We saw this pitfall illustrated most starkly in 2018's The Predator. To a certain extent one could probably argue that there were too many characters in Predator 2 and Predators but those films were at least much more entertaining and efficient than The Predator. Predator 2 also scored points for featuring a lone Predator actually hunting. Prey has clearly studied the franchise and learned important lessons. There aren't too many characters, dialogue is kept to a minimum, there is only one Predator, and the backdrop to the film is a remote wilderness. These were all components of the original 1987 film and all the components that the sequels seemed to stray further and further away from until Prey.

Prey is definitely a return to form after The Predator but it does have some problems. The pacing in the film is too slow in the first half and it takes too long for anything to happen. The CGI animals don't look terribly convincing and Amber Midthunder feels a trifle contemporary for someone living in 1719. Overall though this is a very good film. There is doubtless a temptation, given the success of this film, to do a direct sequel featuring Naru again. My own view is that this isn't necessary. We've done Predator 1719 so let's move on and do a different Predator film next time. Make the franchise an anthology - as it always has been.

Prey drew amazing reviews when it was released to streaming platforms and at 94% has the highest Rotten Tomatoes ranking of any Predator film. You may balk at at that and still consider the original to be the best film in the franchise and that's perfectly fine. I should add that Predator still has a higher audience score than Prey on Rotten Tomatoes. Prey does though have a higher audience score than any movie in the franchise besides the original film. The consensus then is that Prey is the best movie since the original.

Whatever you think of Prey it was nice to see the Predator franchise, so often derided by critics down the years, getting some fairly universal critical acclaim for once. The most important thing about Prey was that its success ensured there would be more Predator films again in the future. It's difficult to rank the Predator films because some of them are so different from one another. Prey and Predator 2 are very different films and The Predator, with its comedic slant, doesn't have much in common with the others.

Predators is sort of similar to the first film in style - only not as good. I'd imagine nearly everyone would have the original Predator film at the top of the pile. Predator 2 is generally considered to be an awful film by many outside Predator fandom but I would actually have Predator 2 in second place in my own list. For pure entertainment value Predator 2 is hard to beat if you ask me. Yes, the film is dated and a bit silly but it's a lot of fun. As for third place, well, I'd probably have Prey taking the edge over Predators - though I'm certainly fond of Predators. As for last place, you probably won't be surprised to hear that I have The Predator at the bottom of pile and by some considerable distance too.

Placing the Alien vs Predator films into the franchise as a whole is not easy. These films don't feel like a true part of the Predator franchise - nor indeed the Alien franchise. The two AvP films feel juvenile and amateurish compared to the best Predator films. Though it pains me to admit this I'd still probably rather watch the first Alien vs Predator film than The Predator! On the whole though I don't think the Alien vs Predator films were a good idea. This concept worked reasonably well in some of the comics but that concept was too compromised in the films because they didn't have the budget to do anything too ambitious or faithful.

As for the future of the franchise, it seems that the Predator will be like the xenomorph or Michael Myers. A great movie villain that is constantly resurrected. We can only hope that some great Predator films will be made in the future. And, who knows, maybe we'll get a great Predator streaming or TV show one day. As long as it had money and talent behind it that could work.

PREDATOR FAN FILMS

There are a smattering of Predator fan films knocking around. Some of these are unavoidably rough and ready and amateurish but the enthusiasm for the Predator universe always shines through and many of these short films are enjoyable to watch. A few too many of these fan films tend to involve amateur actors wandering around in the woods but there are certainly some very creative and ambitious ones too.

Perhaps the most obvious place to start with fan films is BATMAN: DEAD END. Batman: Dead End is a 2003 short film written and directed by Sandy Collora that premiered at the San Diego Comic-Con. Collora worked as a design artist on films like Jurassic Park, Men In Back, and The Crow, and was also an uncredited design artist on Predator 2. This film generated a lot of buzz on release with Kevin Smith famously calling it the greatest depiction of Batman on screen. Batman: Dead End came in the wake of Joel Schumacher's cartoonish child friendly take on Batman and seemed inspired by Alex Ross. Fans seemed to enjoy seeing a darker more comic book faithful take on Batman and with a grey costume no less (as in the comics). As if that wasn't enough, the film also throws in some Predators and xenomorphs.

Batman: Dead End starts with Batman (Clark Bartram) suiting up because the Joker (Andrew Koenig) has escaped from Arkham. Not the most original start to the film but it is quite novel and refreshing to see Batman suiting up in a gray cloth costume as opposed to the black rubber muscle suit that the feature films always seem to use. Batman finds the Joker in a rain sodden alley and after a short rumination on the nature of their seemingly forever entwined battles the Joker is snatched by something unseen - which turns out to be one of the xenomorphs from the Alien film series. Batman fights the xenomorph and is saved by the weapon blast of a - shock - Predator! So Batman then has to fight a Predator but just when it seems as if he has the upper hand more Predators and xenomorphs emerge from the darkness.

There's a lot to like in this short film. The Joker is enjoyably comic book (if a trifle hammy) and that image of Batman's huge cape slowly rising from the puddle is fantastic. It's nice to see Batman in a gray suit for once and Collora proves that they probably could have made the gray costume work in a feature film. The Predators and xenopmorphs are not bad for such a low budget feature and there's a nice effect when the Joker is snatched by the alien and is carried away suddenly. Weaknesses of the film? Well, Batman is a trifle tubby and lumbering. It's hard to believe this Batman could really hold his own in a fight with with a xenomorph or Predator!

Still, it's fun anyway when Bats deploys his Bat-Blade to battle the Predator and the film does capture an unmistakable Batman essence that eluded some of the bigger budget films featuring the Caped Crusader. The xenomorphs perhaps aren't quite as effective as the Predators in the film but with a limited budget and time it's probably hard to capture the ferocity of these famous creatures. Batman ends up grappling with one as if he's in a wrestling match and anyone who has watched one of the Alien films will know this is most unlikely! Collora never managed to follow through on the buzz generated by this film and did not make the leap into features. His next effort, World's Finest, a fan film trailer for a fictitious film starring Batman and Superman, was cheesy and amateurish. Batman: Dead End is a nice little fan film though and certainly worth a look for Batman, Predator and Alien fans.

PREDATOR: DARK AGES is a 2015 short film by James Bushe. Dark Ages stands out from most of the other Predator fan films because it has some pretty decent acting and also some impressive special effects. The moment in the film where the Predator deploys - to very deadly effect - its shoulder plasma cannon is very nicely done. The plot of the film (which is about 25 minutes long) is set in the medieval era and has a group of Templar knights faced with the threat of the Predator (who the local folks take to be a demon haunting the land). Dark Ages feels like a professional and conventional short for much of its running time rather than a fan film and while they obviously didn't have a huge amount of money up their sleeve the Predator stuff is done well when it arrives.

There are nice shots in Dark Ages of the countryside, a lush score, and a good central performance by Adrian Bouchet. It's hard to say if this premise would have worked in a feature length format but as a short film it works very well. Dark Ages is the most professional of the Predator fan films and is admirable for the way it manages to avoid the amateurish acting and cheesy special effects you tend to take for granted in these sorts of projects. What this short film does illustrate is how there was still a lot of untapped potential for the Predator series in that you have all these different historical time periods to pick from and yet the Predator films always seemed to be set in the present day. Thankfully though, with the success of Prey the Predator franchise was at least able to stretch its wings a bit and do something new.

WARRIOR: PREDATOR is a 2019 short film by Chris R. Notarile in which a Native American woman must fight a Predator. Sound familiar? In this case though there are two Predators and they happen to be sisters! Warrior: Predator is only seven minutes long and while the premise is fun the execution leaves something to be desired. It's mean to be too nitpicky because this is a fan film and Notarile obviously didn't have much money up his sleeve but the two Predators are plainly just two ordinary women wearing masks and the fight scenes are very amateurish. You can't fault the enthusiasm in the fan film though and the locations are nice. You should give Warrior a watch but it is clearly a less professional fan film than some of the more ambitious ones out there like Dark Ages.

AVP REDEMPTION is a 2010 fan film by Alex Popov. This film uses CGI for the backdrops and takes place in the future where the Sulaco (from ship from Aliens) is now used for genetic research. The body of a Predator is brought aboard but it has an alien facehugger inside it - which escapes. News of this reaches the Predators and so they send one of their own to the Sulaco to tidy things up - which basically means kill everything! AvP Redemption is clearly a labour of love and wisely eschews too much acting and exposition to get to the action as quickly as possible. The special effects are decent enough for a fan film and the Predator costumes and scenes are terrific. Some of the shots of the Predator are worthy of a genuine feature film. AvP Redemption has a more exciting and interesting premise than either of the official Alien vs Predator movies and scores points for being set in the future in outer space (as opposed to in the woods on Earth - which is where nearly all of the other Predator fan films seem to be set). AvP Redemption is definitely worth watching if you are a Predator fan.

The YouTube channel Super Beat Down pits famous superheroes and characters against one another to see who might win in a fight between between them. One of the episodes they did featured WOLVERINE V PREDATOR. This segment was very well done with a great Predator costume. The actor playing Wolverine was pretty good too. The thing that makes Wolverine very competitive against a Predator is that he has self healing abilities. Plus of course Wolverine has adamantium claws so can do plenty of damage himself in a fight. This segment is great fun and worth watching.

PREDATOR: CELTIC DAYS is a 2017 fan film by Marcin Skruch. Celtic days is set in Ireland in XVIII c and the plot involves that antique pistol which was given to Harrigan at the end of Predator 2. I enjoyed the campfire scenes but otherwise struggled to get into Celtic Days - which felt a few rungs down from Dark Ages when it comes to Predator fan films set hundreds of years ago. The Predator stuff is fairly minimal and confined to the end and the film is a trifle slow and uninteresting for much of its duration. Celtic Days wasn't really my cup of tea but a lot of effort has obviously gone into this short film so you should definitely take a look.

THE CREATURE FROM THE BIG MOUNTAIN is a Predator fan film by Damien De Bourguignon. This French film is set during World War 2 and features some German soldiers encountering the Predator in the countryside. The Creature From The Big Mountain is shot in black and white and is very nicely done as far as fan films go. it looks professional and the costumes are pretty good. The acting is not bad either. The only nitpick one would have though is that the Predator itself doesn't really look much like a Predator when it finally appears. They obviously couldn't manage to get a very good mask. That quibble aside though The Creature From The Big Mountain is certainly worth a look.

PREDATOR VS COLONIAL MARINES is a 2016 short film by Julian Higgins. This is a very simple fan film which takes place in a warehouse. A group of marines arrive and encounter a Predator. You never see the Predator and the deaths occur offscreen. Though very basic, the short does make you have to use your imagination and the sound effects are good. Predator vs Colonial Marines has a simplicity which sort of works and is at least something different from the usual Predator fan films which feature people wandering around in the woods.

PREDATORS: WORLD WAR is a short fan film by David Melchiorre. This short is set during World War 2 and has an American pilot bailing out in a forest over occupied Europe where he must deal with both friendly and unfriendly factions - plus of course a Predator. World War is one of the most inventive Predator fan films in that although it clearly had a minuscule budget it still looks good - with clever use of stock footage and black and white. What is effective too is the way the film switches to colour for the first gore scene. Another clever thing about World war is that dialogue is kept to a minimum and the story is most told through action and visuals. The acting in short films is obviously not professional so it can take you out of these films if you have some amateur actor with reams of dialogue. What I like about this short film is that, despite the lack of money, it still feels cinematic with plenty of action, some good Predator POV shots, and inventive direction. The actual Predator is not bad either when it finally turns up at the end.

UNTITLED PREDATOR FAN FILM (that's the only title this is listed by) is a nine minute fan film by Kenji Doughty. This film is (again) set during World War 2. A group of American soldiers fighting in the Pacific encounter a Japanese soldier in the jungle. That's the least of their problems though because there is also a (yes, you guessed it) Predator at large. This fan film is perfectly competent and watchable. While the acting is unavoidably hokey, the period military costumes are good and the Predator is not bad at all with a decent Predator mask. They use the score from the first Predator film to drive the action too - which helps. This fan film is generally well done and another creative example of what can be done on a low-budget.

There are a smattering of other Predator fan films but the ones above are the most famous and represent the best efforts. I'd say that out of all the Predator fan films, Batman: Dead End and Dark Ages are the best. AvP Redemption would probably take third spot in my unofficial subjective ranking of the fan films. All of these Predator fan films are very easy to find on YouTube and other places so you should definitely check them all out for yourself if you desire more Predator capers.

PREDATOR VIDEO GAMES

The first ever video game inspired by Predator came out in 1987. This was a licenced game based on the first film. It was made for the Commodore 64 but ported to other machines - including the Amiga in 1989. Licenced games like this were frequently a disappointment for C64 owners. Companies loved to get a movie or television licence because they could slap the film poster on the box and entice gamers to part with their money with alluring cover art alone. A lot of the time though C64 users ended up with a shoddy game for their trouble. Games, for example, based on Big Trouble in Little China and Knight Rider are among the worst C64 games of all time. Caveat emptor was the best advice.

Predator was happily pretty good though and a game that has plenty of atmosphere. In the game you play Arnie's elite special forces character Dutch Schaefer and are dropped into a guerilla festooned jungle. This isn't the only thing in the jungle though. There also happens to be a technologically advanced alien who is on Earth to hunt humans for sport. This game is a side scroller with pretty good graphics. Dutch and the jungle backdrops are both nicely conveyed. The early stages are more generic action fare but then the alien enters the fray - which you become aware of thanks to the screen depicting its laser sights and infra-red vision.

This game is an admirable attempt to capture the spirit and plot of the Predator film and it has a very immersive aura. The flaws in the game are that it's quite short and can be frustratingly difficult. Nonetheless this game deserves a lot of credit for not just taking the licence money and running. They did actually put a lot of effort in here to give you a good game. There are some nice touches too here - like the way you can, as in the film, get Dutch covered in mud to make him less visible to the alien.

It is the level of detail in Predator that is impressive and shows that this wasn't just your bog standard licence grab. I like the way Arnie's character animates when you fire a gun. You really notice little things like this. Predator was a notoriously tricky game and many said they never finshed it but if you are up for a challenge this will certainly test your resolve. I was sort of obsessed with this game for the atmosphere as much as anything. Maybe I was just relieved to finally play a movie tie-in that wasn't dreadful! Predator is a game I have a lot of nostalgia for and - warts and all - this was a memorable experience on the C64 for me.

There were actually two licenced games based on the film Predator 2. Predator 2 is a 1990 game developed by Oxford Mobius and Arc Developments and published by Image Works, Konami and Mirrorsoft for MS-DOS, Amiga, Amstrad CPC, Atari ST, Commodore 64,and the ZX Spectrum. This first version of Predator 2 is an Operation Wolf style rail shooter. Rail shooters were basically the forunner of the FPS genre. You play Harrigan (depicted by a wireframe stick figure) and the screen scrolls past - but with you stuck in a static position. You blast a number of street punks as the mean streets of Los Angeles roll past. This game is rudimentary by today's standards but nostalgic undemanding fun. It's certainly no classic though and doesn't have an awful lot of Predator atmosphere. This version of Predator 2 is really just a generic rail shooter of the era with the predator 2 name slapped over the top.

The second game based on the movie sequel, Predator 2, is a 1992 video game based on the film of the same name. It was developed by Teeny Weeny Games and published by Arena Entertainment for various platforms including Amiga, MS-DOS, and Sega Genesis. The game is a side-scrolling action game sort of like that old arcade game Commando. You race around the streets of Los Angeles as Mike Harrigan blasting baddies and trying to survive encounters with the Predator. Throughout the game, players must complete a series of objectives, such as rescuing hostages or eliminating specific targets.

The levels are set in diverse environments, ranging from city streets to alien-infested spaceships. In addition to combat, players can also utilise stealth tactics and the Predator's cloaking ability to infiltrate enemy strongholds without being detected. Predator 2 has colourful graphics and fast paced gameplay. The game gets a bit samey after a while and can be quite difficult but that spooky alien ship level later on is fun. Predator 2 remains a nostalgic title for fans of the franchise and collectors of retro video games.

Alien vs Predator is a 1993 fighting video game developed by Jorudan and published by Activision for the Super Nintendo Entertainment System (SNES). The game is based on the popular comic franchise of the same name, featuring a crossover between the extraterrestrial species, Alien, and the intergalactic hunters, Predator. In Alien vs Predator, players can choose to play as either an Alien or a Predator character. Each character has their own unique moves, abilities, and playstyle. The game features a single-player mode where players must navigate through various levels, defeating enemies and bosses along the way. There is also a two-player mode that allows players to compete against each other in fights.

The gameplay involves side-scrolling action, with players being able to jump, attack, and perform special moves. The levels are filled with enemies such as other aliens or predators, as well as environmental hazards. Players can collect power-ups and weapons throughout the levels to enhance their abilities and increase their chances of survival.

One notable feature of Alien vs Predator is the ability for the Alien player to wall-crawl and cling to ceilings, while the Predator player can use various hunting tools like the famous retractable wrist blades. Both characters have their own set of unique abilities and attacks, creating different gameplay experiences depending on the chosen character. Alien vs Predator is fun for a while but does a bit headache inducing and samey in the end. Some of the bosses are a trifle annoying too.

Alien vs. Predator is an arcade game released in 1994 by Capcom. It is a beat 'em up game that features characters from the Alien and Predator franchises. The game allowplayers to choose between four different characters: Dutch (from the film Predator), Linn Kurosawa (a new character created for the game), Predator Warrior, and Major Dutch Schaefer (from the film Predator). The gameplay involves players fighting against hordes of enemies, including aliens, predators, and human soldiers. The game also features cooperative multiplayer, allowing two players to play together and defeat the enemies together. It was a popular arcade game during its time and is still beloved by fans of the Alien and Predator franchises. Capcom's Alien vs. Predator is a very polished looking game with lovely crisp graphics and great sound effects.

Alien vs Predator is a first-person shooter game developed by Rebellion Developments and released for the Atari Jaguar console in 1994. In the game, players can choose to control either the Colonial Marine, the Alien, or the Predator. Each character has their own unique abilities and playstyle. As the Colonial Marine, you must navigate through various environments, from the corridors of a space station to alien-infested jungles, while battling both Aliens and Predators. The gameplay focuses on fast-paced action and shooting mechanics, with a heavy emphasis on exploration and survival.

Playing as the Alien offers a different experience, as you can climb walls, crawl on ceilings, and use your deadly claws and tail to attack enemies. You must stealthily move through levels, avoiding detection and silently taking out your targets. Lastly, playing as the Predator allows you to utilize advanced alien technology, including the iconic cloaking device and shoulder-mounted plasma cannon. You can hunt your prey using thermal vision and engage in brutal melee combat. The game features multiple levels set in diverse locations and includes various mission objectives. Players can collect weapons and health pickups, and each character's health and energy are displayed on-screen.

Alien vs Predator on the Atari Jaguar is often praised for its atmospheric visuals, intense gameplay, and faithful representation of the movie franchise. It is considered one of the standout titles on the console and a cult classic among gamers. The game is quite ambitious for 1994 with decent graphics and plenty of atmosphere. So long as you aren't expecting Doom Eternal this game is pretty good. The gameplay is based on then recent FPS games like Wolfenstein and Doom and Alien v Predator received quite positive reviews. While it seems dated today it was perfectly competent for the time.

The game takes place in the Golgotha Training Base of the United States Colonial Marines Corps built by Weyland-Yutani on the Vortigern Sector Perimeter. When an unknown Space Jockey Boneship vessel approaches the base, a Chatterjee Class tug is sent to retrieve it for further examination. As soon as the vessel is aboard on the base, it is quickly overrun by the xenomorphs. The game seems a little slow these days compared to the furious shooting action of the original Doom but the textures and backdrops are quite good and the game does have a commendable sense of atmosphere. When you shoot xenomorphs they explode into a puddle of green acid!

Aliens versus Predator is a science fiction first-person shooter computer game developed by Rebellion Developments and published by Fox Interactive in North America for Microsoft Windows and Mac OS X computers in 1999. This atmospheric and stylish game drew excellent reviews and once again allowed the player to be a marine, xenomorph, or Predator. This felt like an improvement over previous first person shooters based on the Alien franchise and created a genuinely foreboding aura as you made your way through dimly lit corridors with flickering lights or threw flares into the darkness. 'Aliens versus Predator takes the traditional first-person shooter,' wrote GamesPoint in 1999, 'and, instead of attempting to advance the art of interactive storytelling, simply augments the form with new effects and features that affect gameplay in deep, satisfying ways. With its single-minded focus on terrifying the player, the game is something of a one-trick pony. But that one trick is more than adequate to carry an entire game.'

In 2001 there was a sequel to Aliens versus Predator that arrived with the following blurb: 'On planet LV1201, ancient alien ruins have been discovered. The Weyland-Yutani corporation sets up a research facility in the area, to study and unlock the secrets of the excavation. When xenomorphic (alien) eggs are found, Dr. Eisenberg is assigned command of the scientific progress. Weyland-Yutani also hires a band of mercenaries, under the command of discharged General Rykov to act as security of the facility. As time passes, observation pods are set up to observe an artificial xenomorphic hive. The xenomorphs however manage to escape containment and the resulting chaos sends out a distress call, which attracts the attention of the "Predator" alien species, as well as dispatching a colonial marine vessel, the USS Verloc, to render aid. Three intertwined campaigns tell the story: that of human marine Lt. Harrison, a newly hatched xenomorph and a Predator clan leader.' Aliens versus Predator 2 didn't offer anything terribly new in comparison to the first game but more of the same was very welcome nonetheless and the reviews were excellent.

Aliens Versus Predator: Extinction is a real-time strategy game set in the Alien vs. Predator universe. Published by EA Games and developed by Zono Incorporated, the game was released in 2003 for the PlayStation 2 and Xbox consoles. In the game, players take control of three factions: Aliens, Predators, and Colonial Marines. Each faction has its unique strengths, weaknesses, and units, providing a different gameplay experience for each. The Aliens are fast, melee-focused creatures that can rapidly reproduce and overwhelm their enemies. They have various types of Aliens available, such as facehuggers, warriors, and queens. The Predators, on the other hand, are highly skilled hunters. They have a variety of weapons, cloaking abilities, and can even call in orbital strikes. Lastly, the Colonial Marines are the human faction equipped with advanced military technology. They rely on firepower, base building, and defense structures to fight against the other two factions.

The game's single-player campaign includes three separate campaigns, one for each faction, where players complete various missions and objectives. There is also a multiplayer mode that allows players to compete against each other or co-operate against AI-controlled enemies. Aliens Versus Predator: Extinction received mixed reviews from critics. While the concept of playing as different factions from the Alien vs. Predator universe was praised, some critics felt the gameplay mechanics lacked depth and variety. Additionally, the game's graphics and controls were considered to be somewhat lackluster. Despite these criticisms, Aliens Versus Predator: Extinction remains a notable entry in the Alien vs. Predator video game series, offering fans a chance to experience the intense conflict between the iconic alien species and the human military force.

Predator: Concrete Jungle is a third-person action-adventure video game developed by Eurocom and published by Sierra Entertainment. It was released in 2005 for the PlayStation 2 and Xbox consoles. The game is set in a futuristic rendition of New York City in the year 2030. Players assume the role of the Predator, an alien warrior with advanced technology and stealth abilities. The story follows the Predator's mission to eliminate a gang leader named Bruno Borgia, who possesses stolen Predator technology.

The gameplay focuses on stalking and hunting targets, combining stealth, melee combat, and long-range weapons to take down enemies. The Predator has various weapons at its disposal, including the iconic shoulder-mounted plasma cannon, wristblades, a combistick, and smart disc. Players can also make use of the Predator's cloaking technology to remain undetected and perform stealth kills.

As players progress through the game, they can earn upgrades and unlock new abilities and weapons, allowing for more efficient and brutal hunting techniques. The game features both open-world exploration and linear mission-based levels, providing a mix of freedom and structured gameplay. Predator: Concrete

Jungle received mixed reviews from critics. While praised for its faithful depiction of the Predator character and its atmospheric cityscape setting, it was also criticized for its repetitive gameplay and lackluster graphics. Aliens vs Predator: Requiem was a 2007 game exclusive to the PlayStation Portable, developed by Rebellion Developments and published by Vivendi Games. This third-person action-adventure game follows the plot of the film and has the player as a Predator. The game got terrible reviews - just like the film!

Alien vs. Predator is a 2010 first-person shooter video game developed by Rebellion Developments and published by Sega. It is a remake of the 1999 game of the same name and features three playable campaigns, each following the perspective of a different species: the Aliens, the Predators, and the Colonial Marines. The game is set on the planet BG-386, where a group of Colonial Marines have discovered an ancient pyramid beneath an outpost. Unbeknownst to them, the planet is home to both xenomorphs (Aliens) and predators who have been using it as a hunting ground for years.

Each campaign offers a unique gameplay experience. Playing as the Colonial Marines, players must survive hordes of xenomorphs while completing mission objectives. The Predator campaign allows players to utilise the predator's advanced weaponry, stealth, and hunting skills to eliminate their prey, including humans and xenomorphs. Finally, the Alien campaign allows players to control a xenomorph, utilising their agility, speed, and ability to climb walls and ceilings to stalk and kill their prey.

The game's multiplayer mode features various modes, including team deathmatch, capture the flag, and survival, where players can choose to play as either the Aliens, Predators, or Colonial Marines, each with their own unique abilities and playstyles. Aliens vs. Predator received mixed to positive reviews upon release. Critics praised the game's atmospheric environments, detailed graphics, and the faithful adaptation of the Alien and Predator franchises. However, some criticised the game's lack of innovation and relatively short campaign lengths.

This game failed to repeat the critical success of the earlier Alien v Predator games and met with a lukewarm reception. 'The Marine campaign is sometimes absurdly difficult,' wrote the AV Club. 'Guns are forever running out of ammunition. And even though you're facing a creature with acid blood, two tiers of teeth, and daggers for fingers, you're bizarrely encouraged to fight it via mêlée attacks. Whenever an alien gets within 15 feet of you, onscreen prompts instruct you to use a combination of the left and right bumpers to block or strike. Thanks to the surrounding dark, more often than not, you have no idea who or what you're fighting, and wind up flailing wildly at the darkness. In the wake of the difficult Marine campaign, the alien and Predator campaigns offer some much-needed table-turning catharsis. Yet neither ever manages to transcend novelty. All three campaigns overlap, though the Rashômon-like possibilities are never fully explored. The always-terrific Lance Henriksen is on hand to put a human face on—and lend some soul to—this otherwise soulless experience. Yet in the end, his character turns out to be just as hollow as the videogame he's starring in.'

Predator: Hunting Grounds is a multi-player online video game developed by IllFonic and published by Sony Interactive Entertainment. The game is set in the Predator universe and allows players to choose between playing as the Predator or as part of an elite four-person fireteam that is tasked with completing various missions in a hostile jungle environment. As the Predator, players have access to advanced weaponry, stealth abilities, and thermal vision, allowing them to stalk their human prey.

The Predator's goal is to hunt down and eliminate the members of the fireteam one by one, using their superior strength and advanced technology. On the other hand, players can also choose to play as a member of the fireteam, which is armed with a variety of weapons and equipment to defend themselves against the Predator. The fireteam's objective is to complete various missions, such as collecting intel or eliminating hostile forces, all while trying to survive the Predator's relentless pursuit. The game features both competitive and cooperative gameplay, with players being able to form squads and take on missions together as a fireteam. It also offers a progression system, allowing players to unlock new weapons, gear, and abilities as they level up.

PREDATOR COMICS

There are a lot of Predator comics - too many in fact to mention all of them. Some of them are a waste of time and it did all get a bit silly in the end with some of the crossovers too but there are some decent ones out there. The depiction of the Predators in the comics never really seems to do them justice. Too often they are drawn and inked to be too cartoonish and colourful and the Predators remove their helmets too soon and too often - which is a bugbear of mine in some of the films too. I think the Predators have more mystique and menace if they keep their helmets on for longer. It's not as if these helmet masks are purely for show. They do have some tech and optical tricks in them!

Another silly thing about some of the Predator comics is the way humans can fight them bar room brawl style. This depowers the Predators. If you tried to have a fistfight with the Predator from the first two films you'd last about two seconds before losing your spinal cord. It would be like Mike Tyson vs Marvis Frazier. Predator: Concrete Jungle is a four-issue mini-series written by Mark Verheiden, with art by Chris Warner and Ron Randall. As far as the Predator comics go this is where it all began. The story follows the Predator as it stalks its prey on the mean streets of New York City. The Predator has come to Earth to hunt the most dangerous game: humans. It begins a killing spree that attracts the attention of Detective John Schaefer, the brother of Dutch Schaefer, the protagonist of the original Predator film.

Detective Schaefer is determined to put an end to the Predator's reign of terror, but as he delves deeper into the case, he discovers that there is more to these killings than meets the eye. Schaefer is also searching for his missing brother Dutch. Concrete Jungle is a fairly enjoyable comic with simple vibrant art and plenty of action. It is basically a cop thriller like Predator 2 but Schaefer does visit the jungle too to search for Dutch and this allows the story to riff on the first Predator film with the jungle action.

There's quite a nice idea in here too when a character puts on the Predator mask and can suddenly see dozens of cloaked Predator ships above New York. This was obviously stolen from the film They Live but it makes for some arresting panels. Concrete Jungle gets a bit silly and convoluted at times and it isn't very realistic or plausible the way Detective Schaefer is constantly killing Predators and having fights with them but as long as you don't take it too seriously then Concrete Jungle is readable enough. Some of the dialogue is bit hokey but then that's probably to be expected. I think Verheiden did better work on the Alien comics at this time but Concrete Jungle is quite good fun.

In 1991, Detective John Schaefer returned in the comic Predator: Cold War (which was again written by Mark Verheiden). In this story there is Predator activity in Soviet Siberia and Schaefer is forced by the authorities to go and investigate. The Soviets are also investigating this incident and send Lieutenant Valentina Ligachev to lead a team. Ligachev has encountered the Predators before. In the end Schaefer and Ligachev become friends and allies and team up to fight the Predators together. Cold War is a decent enough follow up to Concrete Jungle and it wisely moves away from the New York police thriller angle to become a more horror themed story which, with its isolated snow glazed backdrops, riffs quite a lot on John Carpenter's The Thing. Cold War is generally entertaining - if rather ludicrous at the best of times. The dialogue is nothing to write home about but the story is fun and there is plenty of gore and Predator action too.

In 1996 there was a third John Schaefer story - again by Mark Verheiden. This was called Predator: Dark River. In this story, John Schaefer hears from a pilot that Dutch might be alive and so travels to the jungle to investigate. He's soon mixed up in more danger and mayhem involving Predators, criminals, and the villain General Phillips. Dark River has a few too many plot threads and characters for its own good and it's a bit ridiculous that John Schaefer can constantly have fistfights with Predators and survive but if you liked the first two John Schaefer comics you should find this readable. There is plenty of action and explosions. The story in the comic says that when Dutch was rescued in the helicopter at the end of Predator he was found to have an alien infection so they promptly dumped him back in the jungle! You keep waiting for Dutch to turn up in the comic but he never does.

The Alien and Predator comics eventually, of course, hit upon the idea of pitting the xenomorphs against Predators and so was born Aliens vs Predator. The comic book series for this dates back to 1989. The story begins on Ryushi, a far distant planet that has only just recently been colonised by humans. Ryushi is a sun baked desert planet with nineteen hours of daylight and run by the Chigusa Corporation (this comic derives from that period of history when America seemed slightly paranoid that Japan was on the verge of becoming the greatest economic superpower in the world and would probably run just about everything in the future - including space). The smallish colony on the arid planet is made up mostly of ranchers and cowboy types who raise quadrupedal ungulates called rhynth (basically Alien cows one might say) for export. It's a lucrative business apparently and Ryushi looks a lot like a landscape in a Western film - albeit one with two suns and mountains that have a strange pink hue.

What the Chigusa Corporation and the colonists on the planet don't know though is that Ryushi has been used by the Predators as a hunting ground for many centuries. We learn that the Predators have been traversing the galaxy and seeding planets with alien eggs in order to give them lethal and challenging game reserves worthy of their legendary and ruthless hunting abilities. These Predators do need to find some new hobbies I think! They should try staying in one night with a cup of tea and relaxing.

One of the planets they seed alien eggs on (via a remote control shuttle of some sort that lands undetected by the colony sensors in the desert) is Ryushi. When the alien eggs infect one of the rhynth (the weird cows in case you've forgotten already) it becomes a host for an Alien Queen.

Carnage quickly ensues and the planet soon has a virtually unstoppable infestation of aliens. The only sure defence against the aliens is probably to be on a different planet. When the Predators show up to hunt the aliens the human colonists are now caught in the middle of this vicious interstellar skirmish and a three way battle breaks out. But the Predators were unaware that an Alien Queen was left here by their shuttle and they might have bitten off more than they can chew just for once. They may even need some human assistance despite their natural inclination to hunt us for sport.

The art in Aliens vs Predator is not always spellbinding but this is an entertaining enough comic that fans of these famous cinematic characters and comics in general should enjoy. There are different artists and writers involved as you work your way through and so unfortunately the collection never really has the same atmosphere throughout and often feels quite different from one story to the next. Sometimes the art is slightly random in its structure and then elsewhere it will be very traditional like an old fashioned weekly comic. The art in the Aliens individual comic titles is better to be honest but are some striking and enjoyable flourishes here.

The central character in Aliens vs Predator (and essentially the Sigourney weaver of the comic) is Machiko Noguchi, the Chigusa Corporation's administrator. She begins the story as the corporate boss in a business suit, completely detached and aloof from the planet and workers she has been sent to preside over. Noguchi can't seem to put her stamp on Ryushi and make any connection to the ranchers but all of this changes when the aliens and Predators arrive. Noguchi helps to save the life of a Predator named Broken Tusk and is given the mark of his clan out of respect. She becomes an action heroine. So the Predators now treat her with respect and she becomes like an adopted Predator, living with them and becoming a part of their hunting expeditions.

Noguchi has a story arc that makes Halo Jones look dull. Further story arcs involve the investigation of the loss of the colony on Ryushi by soldiers from Earth and a stand-off with the Predators - with Noguchi caught in the middle between her adopted race and her true species. The comic is not Alan Moore quality in terms of subtext and depth but it does quite a nice job of introducing some interesting themes about loyalty and what it means to be human. The art in the first part of the story seems very old fashioned (it becomes much glossier and more modern feeling in later arcs) but one never really dislikes any of it. There is a nice splash page in particular of a desert scene on the colony, the two suns high in the sky and the skeleton of a rhynth sitting on rocks. Some of the architecture of the colony is a nice riff on James Cameron's Aliens. The Aliens vs Predator action - when it finally arrives - is a lot of fun.

The Predator shuttle making its ay through the atmosphere of the colony to deliver its deadly payload is done in an entertaining 'three panel down the page' format with splodgy yellow vapour trails adding a pleasantly psychedelic tint to the page. The sun baked location is a nice contrast to the cold metallic spaceships and dark corridors of the films. One of the fun sections here is a black and white prologue of the Predators leaving alien eggs on a planet (where the curious wildlife soons falls victim to the facehuggers) and then returning to hunt aliens in what appears to be a giant swamp.

They even have what looks to be a younger Predator with them being taught the rules of the hunt. The whole sequence (which lasts for several pages) is juxtaposed with bored computer programmers on Ryushi sitting in a control room and pondering how their job is one that anyone could do. They don't really feel alive or do anything that gets their heart pumping and go into something of a rant against technology. One of the most interesting things about this comic is the way that it provides more background to the Predators and their traditions. They might be intergalactic serial killers who live to kill things but the comic always makes them seem quite noble with their own codes and sense of honour. They are a warrior society where everything revolves around hunting prowess and being the strongest and most determined. One of the best stories simply involves a Predator hunt and features little or no dialogue.

Aliens vs Predator is an entertaining read if you are a fan of the characters although it isn't something that sticks in the memory for too long and is something you just enjoy at the time rather than a classic comic that you would return to again and again. This is not The League of Extraordinary Gentlemen or The Dark Knight Returns. It isn't as gruesome as you might expect although the language is occasionally a little crude and might be unsuitable for younger readers.

Batman versus Predator is a 1991 comic book crossover by Dark Horse Comics written by Dave Gibbons with art by Andy Kubert. This is the best of the Predator crossover stories and works better than you might expect. The story begins with a big local heavyweight boxing match in Gotham City with both participants backed by different shady and powerful underworld crime figures - Alex Yeager and Leo Brodin. Later that night the winning boxer of the contest is brutally murdered ('Marks on his body look like a net was used. Cut him to the bone then his head and spinal column were removed') in his apartment, leading Batman and the police to suspect and fear that a nasty gang war between rival mobsters and their crews is now on the cards with Brodin, gangster backer of the losing boxer, the chief suspect for the murder. The police and Batman are puzzled and somewhat troubled though by the unnecessarily grisly and gruesome nature of the killing. 'Who'd Brodin hire for the hit? Jack the Ripper?' muses Jim Gordon's assistant.

The mayor of Gotham duly organises a summit between the rival gangsters in an attempt to calm matters before they get out of hand but the meeting is gatecrashed by a huge, shadowy, almost invisible figure armed with elaborate weaponry who creates yet more bloody havoc and destruction. With some old fashioned detective work in his high-tech lab and the help of butler Alfred, Batman tracks down the mysterious killer to a junkyard hideout but barely escapes with his life when he is discovered and engages the Predator in a brutal fight. With the help of his remote controlled Batmobile he somehow makes it back to Wayne Manor where Alfred places him comatose in the Batcave's medical unit. As this apparently unstoppable and uncatchable killer continues his violent killing spree, Batman lies injured, presumed dead, and the National Guard is called in ready to sweep the streets unless Batman answers the Bat signal by a certain time. This will produce yet more casualties, something everyone is well aware of while they await any signs that the city's greatest protector is still alive. 'Our killer,' muses a groggy Batman. 'I don't believe it's of this world. I think it's on safari here in Gotham...' Has The Dark Knight finally met his match?

One of the more critically well received of the numerous crossover comic book stories, Batman versus Predator sounds ludicrous on the face of it but is a surprisingly dark and violent piece of art with a decent story that - while a tad derivative - does the job reasonably well. The alien Predators are essentially intergalactic big game hunters and when one pitches up in Gotham it immediately starts picking off who it (sometimes slightly erroneously) assumes are the most powerful people - or 'prey' - available, like the city's two most famous heavyweight boxers and its most salient crime lords. The biggest prey in Gotham though is of course Batman who faces his biggest ever challenge and may even be completely out of his depth.

The art by Andy Kubert is deliberately muddy here with very few bright colours used which, on the plus side, helps to make the infra-red point of view perspectives and laser beams of the Predator much more striking and fun when they are deployed. The story seems to take place entirely in the dark with rain often splattering down on the gothic architecture of Gotham. While it was probably sensible to go for this approach - the Predator would have fitted less comfortably into a brightly lit world of spangly costumed superheroes - if I had a criticism it would be that occasionally I found it a little difficult to actually follow what was happening with all the dark blues, grey and black and had to skim over certain pages more than once.

The Predator is certainly well drawn and enjoyably violent in the story, leaving some gruesome carnage for the police and Batman to find. For a while the authorities are puzzled by the nature of the killer and it becomes known as The Slasher, an invisible or 'see-through' killer that is slowly but steadily making the streets of Gotham no go areas. The story arc has Batman soundly beaten by his first encounter with this extraterrestrial Alan Quartermein and forced to recuperate bed-ridden in the safety of the Batcave while the killing spree goes on outside. When he asks Alfred how he is, his faithful butler replies, 'Rather poorly I'm afraid sir. Deep puncture wounds, extensive lacerations, third degree burns and severe concussion. You're lucky to be alive.'

This sets the scene for a climatic and much bigger showdown between Batman and the Predator which is somewhat reminiscent of the final act of Frank Miller's The Dark Knight Returns and also contains a few nods to the Predator films made by John McTiernan and Stephen Hopkins in the eighties and early nineties. Predator 2 in particular with its urban city environment seems to be a big influence here. In this universe other more high powered DC superheroes don't seem to exist - or at least are not mentioned - which is a wise move I feel. The personal and daunting nature of the challenge Batman faces to protect the people of his city is therefore heightened, something that obviously wouldn't be the case if it was possible to just telephone The Justice League or Superman. Batman is really a loner who relies on his courage, wits and ingenuity rather than special powers and Batman versus Predator is aware of this.

While the story veers towards the predictable at times in Batman versus Predator there are some nice moments that lift this slightly above the more straight ahead and daft cash-in crossovers. I enjoyed seeing Batman have to do some detective work - he tracks down the Predator's hideout by analysing metal rust flakes in his lab - and also deploys his technological expertise to make himself more of a match for the equally technologically minded Predator. The final showdown between the pair is certainly entertaining with a coda that supplies another nod to one of the Predator films. There were two sequels to Batman v Predator and while neither was as good as the first one they are still worth reading.

Another fun crossover comic is Judge Dredd v Predator by John Wagner. In this story the Predator goes hunting in Mega City One and meets his match in the no nonsense future lawman. There were a huge amount of crossover comics like this. One of the most bizarre is Tarzan v Predator. This comic is a bit silly at the best of times but it's sort of fun because if anyone would stand a chance of surviving in a jungle with a Predator it is surely Tarzan!

Predator: Hell Come a Walkin' is a two-issue limited comic book series that was first published by Dark Horse Comics from February-March 1998. It was written by Nancy A. Collins, illustrated and colored by Dean Ormston. In this story Union and Confederate soldiers encounter a Predator during the Civil War. The main hero in this comic is Jesse James. Predator: Hell Come a Walkin' is decent enough as a period Predator yarn and has some of the best depictions of the Predators in any comic. The Predators often come off as cartoonish and even slightly silly in comic books but the drawings of them here are pretty good and quite realistic. They manage to retain their darkness and mystique in this comic - which is high praise indeed.

Superman vs. Predator is 2001 crossover by David Michelinie and Alex Maleev. In the story a spaceship is discovered by S.T.A.R. Labs in the jungle and Superman goes to investigate. It turns out to be a Predator ship and mercenaries are soon on the scene. They work for the villain - a scientist who plans a genocide in order to reshape humanity. Or something like that. Predators show up and there's an underground pyramid which anticipates the first AvP film.

Anyway, why would any of this be trouble for Superman? Well, it turns out that contact with the Predator ship has given Superman some sort of virus so he spends the story weakened. This is exactly the sort of thing they did in the Superman/Aliens crossover. A convenient plot device to make the Predators a match for Superman. Superman vs. Predator is quite a dull comic with stratchy art. It takes far too long for the Predator action to arrive and the story is a bit convoluted with all the stuff concerning the grand scheme of the Bond style villain. Superman vs. Predator is only really for the very curious and not the most exciting Predator comic you will encounter.

Superman and Batman versus Aliens and Predator is a 2007 crossover by Mark Schultz. Superman and Batman had both already encountered the xenomorphs and Predators in previous adventures but here they do so together. This yarn takes places in the Andes. It comes to light that a group of Predators crashed on Earth hundreds of years ago and set up an underground society near a volcano. They brought alien eggs with them so there are also xenomorphs.

Superman decides to help the Predators escape because the volcano is about to blow but the military is also aware of this alien presence and plans to nuke the area. Batman and Superman must team up to get these aliens off the planet before the missiles arrive. Superman and Batman versus Aliens and Predator is a rather silly comic with that glossy 'realistic' art (sort of like Kingdom Come but less stylish) which I don't care for too much for in comics. Superman doesn't really work in a Predator story because he's too powerful. The Predators can't fight or hurt Superman. In fact, in the story they take him to be a God because he can fly.

Predator: Big Game is a four-issue comic book miniseries

published by Dark Horse Comics in 1991. It was written by John Arcudi and illustrated by Evan Dorkin. Big Game revolves around Corporal Enoch Nakai, a young Native American Indian serving at an army base in New Mexico. A Predator spaceship is recovered nearby by the military but as they try to make sense of this strange craft it soon becomes apparent that a dangerous entity is at large in the area. Big Game is generally very entertaining with colourful art and plenty of gore. The tone is a bit all over the place and some of the humour doesn't land but overall it's a fun undemanding read.

Predator: Xenogenesis is a four issue comic by Ian Edginton which came out in 1999. The premise of the comic is that a special team of mercenaries with futuristic weapons is tasked with turning the tables on the Predators and wiping them out. This comic is not as fun to read though as that premise makes it sound. The story is somewhat confusing in places and the very cartoonish art definitely won't be for all tastes. Predator: Race War is a five-issue limited comic book series that was first published by Dark Horse Comics from February-October 1993. The story was written by Andrew Vachss and Randy Stradley. Race War has a great premise in that the Predator stalks a high security prison in order to kill a serial killer.

Predator: Captive is a one-shot comic book that was first published by Dark Horse Comics in May 1998. It was written by Gordon Rennie. The premise of Captive is that a billionaire named Tyler Stern who likes owning rare objects has done the impossible and captured a Predator - which he keeps captive in a huge biosphere. Stern even supplies the Predator with humans to hunt. He hopes that once the predator accepts that it can't escape it will begin communicating with him. Well, as you might imagine, keeping a Predator captive is surely like asking for trouble. Captive is an interesting and something different from the run of mill Predator stories. It is certainly worth a look.

Aliens vs. Predator: Eternal is a four-issue limited comic book series that was first published by Dark Horse Comics from June-

September 1998. It was written by Ian Edginton, illustrated by Alex Maleev and colored by Perry McNamee and Dan Jackson. In the story a tech billionaire named Gideon Suhn Lee has lived for centuries thanks to harvesting Predator organs from a crashed ship. The alien tech was of course what built his empire. Gideon is now becoming mortal and so is trying to lure and capture Predators to prolong his life.

A journalist named Becka McBride ends up investigating Gideon and gets mixed up in the Predator mayhem. Not just Predator mayhem too because alien eggs are thrown into the story too - leading to xenomorph trouble. Eternal has quite an interesting story - though one that always promises more than it delivers. There is quite a good setpiece here when the xenomorphs get loose in the Tokyo sewer system and Predators move in. There is plenty of action and the comic is always quite interesting but it does fizzle out a bit in the end and you occasionally find yourself losing track of who is who. The story here though is better than the one used in either of the AvP movies.